Thrill the body...

GREAT
IN BED

...blow the mind

Thrill the body...

GREAT IN BED

...blow the mind

Debby Herbenick, PhD
and **Grant Stoddard**

LONDON, NEW YORK, MUNICH,
MELBOURNE, DELHI

Editor Salima Hirani
Designer & Retoucher Miranda Harvey

Project Editors Daniel Mills and
Laura Palosuo
Project Art Editor Charlotte Seymour
Managing Editor Penny Smith
Managing Art Editor Marianne
Markham
Jacket Designer & Illustrator
Charlotte Seymour
Senior Production Editor Jennifer Murray
Production Controller
Alexandra Beeden
Creative Technical Support
Sonia Charbonnier
Publisher Peggy Vance

Published in the United States in 2012 by
DK Publishing, 375 Hudson Street,
New York, New York 10014

11 12 13 14 15 10 9 8 7 6 5 4 3 2 1
001—180694—Jan/2012

A catalog record for this book is
available from the Library of Congress.

ISBN 978-0-7566-8966-7

Printed and bound in Singapore by
Tien Wah Press

Discover more at www.dk.com

Between the covers

Introduction

Most people aim to be good at the things they do. A few select individuals aim their sights higher, seeking out knowledge from experts and practicing for hours to develop jaw-dropping skills. Fortunately for you and your present or future partners, becoming a highly pleasing bedmate appears to be important to you or else you wouldn't be reading this book. After all, why be good in bed when you can be great?

There is, of course, a great deal at stake: the happiness and satisfaction of you and your partners, the vibrancy and harmony of a long-term relationship, not to mention your reputation as a guaranteed good time in the sack. (There's nothing more ego-plumping than a sex referral.) In *Great in Bed* we've striven to give you all the information you need to exceed your wildest expectations as well as those of anyone lucky enough to roll around with you.

No stone unturned In our attempts to impart the very best sex advice, we've taken a comprehensive approach. While there's oodles of scientific and anecdotal advice on the, ahem, nuts and bolts of sex, we've also delved into the peripheral and too-often overlooked aspects of getting it on. Here in these pages you will find information on the importance of becoming intimately familiar with your own parts and in so doing discovering what works for you; exploring your deepest and most titillating fantasies and creating a mental checklist of your turn-ons and offs; being seductive while being yourself; tips for getting what you want without having to employ social dynamics, neurolinguistic programming, or pheromones; receiving feedback on your performance and appraising a partner's; and of course finding ways to marry safer sex and pleasure together in the most harmonious of ways.

You, me, and everyone we know *Great in Bed* holds the keys to better sex for singles, couples, and threesomes, as well as those who are dating or trying their best at mating. It's written for both men and women, adults of all ages, and certainly an array of sexual orientations. It's also written for people of a variety of experience levels. Beginners will find clear instructions for how to get in the game and seasoned; experimental types will discover new ways to seduce, please, and be pleased.

> "Being truly great in bed may require hour upon hour of practice. It's tough, of course, but we know you can do it"

At your service One of your guides, **Dr. Debby Herbenick**, is a sexual research scientist and sex educator at Indiana University and the famed Kinsey Institute. Throughout *Great in Bed*, you'll find important information about the latest that sexual science has to offer, from how many people engage in certain sex

"We like to think that what goes around comes around— put **great sex** out there and great sex will fall in your path"

acts to some of the greatest predictors of men's sexual satisfaction.

Your other guide on this journey, **Grant Stoddard**, has made a career out of reporting directly from the sexual trenches through his first-person accounts of things that would make you blush if you weren't so committed to becoming fantastic in bed yourself. Grant gleaned his know-how not through the rigors of the scientific method but via trial and error so you don't have to. At least, not quite as much.

What the doctor ordered Implement the wisdom we impart in the pages of this book and get used to hearing things like "Wow!", "Where did you learn to do that?", and "Who the hell *are* you?" You'll soon find that being great in bed has all kinds of positive ramifications beyond you and your partner(s) having fun in the sack. Having mind-blowing sex will probably make you feel less stressed, more relaxed, imbue you with a more positive outlook on life, and have you feeling more confident and comfortable in your own skin. Furthermore, fully satisfying sex can be an immune system booster, a pain reliever, and can improve your overall health and well-being. Seminal plasma contains zinc, calcium, and other minerals shown to hinder tooth decay. That's right: A blow job a day may keep the dentist away (unless, of course, playing dentist is your thing… role playing is also a part of being great in the sack for some).

A greater quality of sex will almost certainly lead to a greater quantity of sex, and pretty soon you'll find that all that calorie-burning bumping is making you both look and feel better than ever. Your bed may just be the best piece of exercise equipment ever invented!

Staying safe While there's a long list of positive outcomes from having lots of great sex, sexually transmitted infections and unwanted pregnancies present some pretty significant bummers. Having safer sex absolutely doesn't have to get in the way of all the fun you'll be having. In fact, we stress that knowing that you've been responsible between the sheets (or in a hotel elevator) will enhance your enjoyment overall by reducing worries. Ultimately, having safer sex means having more and better sex.

How to become great in bed

First things first Well, to start with, you have to get into bed, ideally with someone else. As such, the first part of this book features a wealth of information about catching a potential partner's eye, flirting with them, planning a date, making your move, and getting them, if not into, at least into the vicinity of a bed. And when you're there, we talk you through kissing like a pro.

Foreplay = more play Once you and the object of your affection are finally in bed together, your journey to greatness continues with our well-earned suggestions about using foreplay to arouse your partner and prepare for exciting and possibly orgasmic sex. We're talking kissing, caressing, breast play, touching your parts and their parts, and all those exciting moments of early sex exploration. We give you the ins and outs of her body, his body, and how all the bits and pieces fit together. Nipples? Check. Butts? Oh yes. We also share unique information with you on how important it is to embrace the awesomeness of penises and vulvas and the fantastic things they can do (being a memorable sexer most certainly involves being decisive about the riveting nature of these parts). Nor have we left out the sensual ways that the best bedmates learn to explore touching, licking, sucking, or even nibbling each other's backs, thighs, chests, necks, and toes.

A custom-made sex life Learning to be great—even fantastic—in bed requires an education in asking for it in the nicest ways and the naughtiest ways. No matter your level of comfort when it comes to dirty talk, we have something for you. *Great in Bed* is nothing if it isn't about helping you to create a tailor-made sex life that works within your comfort zone while helping you step just enough outside of it that you raise the bar and have better sex than you previously thought was possible.

Getting it on Of course, we also have a plethora of sex positions. Some of them you may have tried before but a good number of them may be new to you—and we highly recommend that you try them again and again, and with gusto. Not to mention some water-based lubricant or one of the many sex toys (vibrators, dildos, whips, clamps, etc.) sprinkled throughout this sex guide. We hope that even if you're no slouch in the bedroom, you'll give this book a read and still find oodles of tidbits to improve your game. The way we have sex is constantly changing, definitions of what sex is are ever expanding, and staying on top of its permutations is critical in keeping the sex you and your partners have fun, fresh, and exciting.

So congratulations! You are 183 pages away from being great (or even greater) in bed. Remember that with great power comes great responsibility. Use it wisely. Or not. Either way.

Chapter 1
From dating to mating

Thrilling *date venues*

From candlelit meals to Ferris wheels You've expressed mutual interest, exchanged numbers, and arranged a rendezvouz. What you've got yourself is a hot date. During this crucial window of opportunity, you'll want to signal that, in addition to being charming company in a social setting, you're also a veritable phenomenon in the sack, and you'll be looking for similar indicators in the other person, too.

Where you go and what you do on a first date is integral to effectively sizing each other up and making an informed, adult, and conscientious decision about getting nasty.

Here are three words to think about when selecting a date venue or activity: Excitation Transfer Theory. Any guy who's ever given a girl a ride on the back of a motorcycle can attest to its potency. The theory posits that if you share an exhilarating experience with somebody—a ride on a roller coaster or pulling a prank on a stranger—the other person will begin to transfer the rush of visceral excitement from the activity itself to you[1]. You don't have to engage in something risky to benefit from ETT. Just exposing the other person to novel stimuli should be enough to prime them—and you— for naughtier fun. So with that in mind...

The dinner date Dinner is a solid date format because, a lot of the time, it does the trick. Eating at a restaurant gets you opposite one another for an hour or two, sharing a fairly intimate, sensory, and hopefully pleasurable experience. Foreshadowing! Precisely because going out for dinner is such a tried-and-tested date itinerary, you'll stand out from the crowd (and increase your chances of getting lucky) by playing with the concept and devising an evening that's more exhilarating and memorable. Instead of a sit-down dinner, seek out a private

If you share *an exhilarating experience,* the other person will begin to **transfer the excitement to you**

cheese-and-wine party. Not only are delicate little bites and sips more sexy and novel than a drawn out, rib-sticking dinner, you'll also be describing the bouquets, flavors, and textures to one another, surreptitiously getting yourselves thinking about other pleasurable sensations. Another less-ordinary dining experience might be at a restaurant where you play a participatory role in the preparation of your meal. Korean barbecue, shabu-shabu, even fondue—if you

COMPILE AN EXCITING-FIRST-DATE-VENUES LIST Even before there's a prospect of a date it pays to have a list of venue possibilities. If you **hear of something fun**, cool, or novel going on, **email or text it to yourself so you don't forget it**. Then, when you want to propose getting together, you won't have to scramble around trying to think of something interesting, draw a blank, and end up in an arbitrary, nondescript chain restaurant. It happens to the best of us.

have the cojones to add a little après-ski kitsch. Unstuffy, etiquette-be-damned activity dinners are great for dissipating first-date jitters and getting stuck into the matter at hand. Blind-dining, a relatively new restaurant concept, in which diners eat blindfolded or in a completely dark room, allows you to engage your taste buds in a different way and pre-excite the pleasure receptors. Definitely worth considering.

Unstuffy, *etiquette-be-damned* activity dinners are great for **dissipating first-date jitters**

Introducing your date, or being introduced by them, to some esoteric, unassuming dive that's famous for a particular item (a sublime sandwich, a tasty taco, delectable dim sum, phenomenal pho) can be a lot of fun. Similarly, taking them on a street-food sampler that's part walking tour, part tasting menu, is a great way of arousing his or her intrigue and simultaneously showcasing your impressive in-the-know credentials.

Day dates—brunch, picnics, and so on—can be fun but nighttime is sexier for many reasons, so keep any presex dates to after dark.

Other first-date venues Movies and concerts can be fun but aren't always ideal for early dates, as the main attraction diverts the attention away from one another and onto something else for extended periods of time. You'll be much better off finding some atmospheric, tucked-away cocktail lounge that speaks of your savoir faire, or even a bar where you can engage one another in a game of pool, darts, or shuffleboard.

Dancing, of course, has been the perfect preamble to sex for thousands of years. You can put a novel spin on this activity by forgoing the

megaclub and finding something a little more unconventional. A steamy Brazilian samba club or a Jamaican dance hall night can be new and exciting places to get up close and personal with one another.

Ice skating, roller skating, bowling, canoeing, indoor rock climbing, or riding the bumper cars at a fairground are all great ways to get close to each other while sharing a few thrills and spills, but without having to get too wacky. Make sure that, whatever you end up doing, it is something you genuinely enjoy. Seeing you get all enthusiastic about an activity will be endearing as well as hint at how exuberant you might be later on...

What to say *on a hot date*

Witty anecdotes, conversation starters, sleek pick-up lines Forget canned lines, well-worn jokes, or amusing anecdotes that are designed to showcase what a fun person you are to be around. The single most important and effective thing you can do to have a winning date chat is to keep asking questions, and be genuinely interested in the responses you elicit.

Angle the spotlight By inquiring about the other person's life, you're demonstrating that you're not only fully present and engaged in the conversation, but also that you're intrigued by them. The quickest way to get in someone's good graces is to make them feel special, that they have something interesting to say.

Put aside your dastardly agenda and focus all your attention on the object of your desire, making them feel as if they are the center of the universe for a few hours. They'll respond favorably to the way you make them feel about themselves and be much more inclined to keep the good times rolling. And while you're listening intently to the things they have to say, you may even discover that the gorgeous person you are sitting opposite might just be the love of your life, or at least someone that you're really pleased to have had the chance to get to know.

If you're not dying to know where your date went to college, take the conversation in a direction that you find more tantalizing and can work with more easily. Try steering the conversation toward positive experiences they've had by asking questions such as "What's the best place you've ever traveled to?" or "What's the most amazing restaurant you've

Make them feel like the *center of the universe* and they'll love how you make them **feel about themselves**

ever eaten at?". If you fear your crush might make you weak at the knees and unable to think of any good questions at the time, have a few prepared in advance to pull out of your sleeve. When you inspire people to recall positive, pleasurable experiences, you subtly encourage them to associate those feelings with you, making it more likely that you'll later

GRANT'S SEXPLOITS For one of my assignments several years ago, I was asked to have a consultation with a dating coach in New York City. We had a mock date in a coffee shop. I thought I'd done fairly well, and was shocked when she gave me a low score. Apparently I'd shown only a perfunctory interest in her career and hobbies. What I took home from that is that you really ought to be genuinely intrigued by someone for the Q-and-A approach to work.

have the chance to show them how accurate such an association is.

Of course, they'll probably want to know a few things about you as well. Without being evasive, answer their questions in a way that's brief, impactful, and intriguing, and then seamlessly put the ball back in their court.

Maintain a balance It sounds counterintuitive, but a little dab of self-deprecating humor can actually help emphasize your attributes when having a flirty chat. The ability to laugh at one's foibles is a very attractive quality, showing that you have the confidence to allow yourself to be vulnerable. Separate studies have shown that while bragging about your own competence, resources, or education will generally have people believing that you're a

When you inspire people to recall *positive, pleasurable experiences*, they **associate those feelings with you**

person who knows what he's doing, there's a trade-off between competence and likability. Throwing in a few self-directed digs, then, means you can have it both ways. You'll get the most mileage out of a self-effacing quip if it comes at the end of a bit of self-serving propaganda. Not only will it soften your boast; it will be an opportunity for you to be humorous and likable.

And relax Lastly, although it can be hard to do on a hot date, try to relax and be your most effervescent self. When people sense that you're nervous, they're more likely to clam up and your hot date will become indistinguishable from a job interview. Keeping a conversational volley going is the key to building a lively, fun, and flirtatious rapport.

May I say *how lovely...*

Be seductive without being desperate or creepy. When we're getting laid good and often, we're confident, chilled, and concentrating (slightly) less on sniffing out sex elsewhere. People pick up on this contentedness and find it extremely alluring. The trick is, then, to project sated joie de vivre even if the only close human contact you've had lately was on a packed bus. These tips will help.

Ditch your expectations Don't put too much stock in a precoital or early date. Check any and all expectations at the door and, as new-agey as it sounds, try to live in the present. Luxuriate in the other person's company, the setting, the drinks, the activity, and your "best self" will shine through. Although a lengthy dry spell can have you believing that you've lost your mojo for good, have faith in the cyclical nature of things and commit to enjoying yourself whether sex is in the cards or not. "Easy come, easy go" is the name of the game here.

Flattery will get you everywhere

There's usually a bit of truth to aphorisms that stand the test of time. If you can make someone feel good about themselves, they'll connect you to that addictive feeling of being appreciated and crave more of it (read: you). It's vitally important to keep compliments specific to them and, of course, genuine. Eyes are a go-to object of flattery, but if he or she has a lazy one, best go for something that's slightly less, um... unique. His or her clothing, sexy voice, or skill with a pool cue are all fair game. It's probably not best practice to compliment him or her on a shapely body part. Even if she's got the sort of bodacious butt you'd like to bury your face in, keep it to yourself until the opportunity to unleash it from her jeans arises.

Subtly gauge their interest

You can be flirty without being overbearing. If you're not sure if he or she is receptive to your charms, try lowering your voice or saying something

> "Some eye contact is good, but unblinkingly staring them down for seconds will, believe it or not, come off as creepy"

conspiratorial. If they aren't shy about leaning in to get their ear closer to your pie hole, there's a pretty good chance that they're open to a bit of flirtatious behavior. You can also change your body posture a few times to see if they mirror your movements—mirroring is an indicator of liking someone.

Once you're pretty sure they're open to it, begin testing the waters by gently touching a knee (if you're sitting) or an arm, to see how they respond. If they reveal something about

themselves that you find amusing, give them a gentle ribbing about it to see if your tease elicits a playful push or verbal volley (both good signs).

Confidence is sexy

By displaying a genuine self-confidence you're letting your date know that, while you're thrilled to be in their company, you don't want or need any validation from them. You can broadcast confidence by taking up some physical space. For guys, this might be standing with the legs shoulder-width apart and adopting an open posture. Women could accentuate their gesticulations. Resist the urge to launch into a monologue about your meteoric rise at work or to drop a reference to your sexual prowess. Instead, whenever appropriate, turn the conversation back to them. They'll soon intuit that you've got nothing to prove and are quite comfortable in your own skin.

Know yourself and be yourself

Anything other than an honest representation of you on a date is going to blow up in your face sooner or later, so don't fake it. If you can't bring yourself to make an actual list, at least think about your strengths and weaknesses from time to time. When you're with company, subtly emphasize the former and be self-deprecating about the latter. Self-awareness is a wonderful quality that shows that you've taken the time to come to terms with your nature.

Date *sparklers*

How to make heads turn, mouths water, loins stir While dressing to impress your date is important, being comfortable is key. When you're getting ready for your big date, think about an outfit that never fails to make you feel fabulous. Your hot date is the time to display the best version of you you've got up your sleeve. No time for self-doubt now. You're gorgeous. It's time to share it!

Guys ZZ Top had it right when they hypothesized that "every girl's crazy about a sharp-dressed man." You can't go too far wrong with a classic, well-fitting blazer or sports coat.

That's not just an opinion, it's evolutionary psychology at work: Women are primed to react positively to a man with a V-shaped torso (wide shoulders, narrow waist) because it's indicative of high levels of testosterone and upper-body strength. For most of our evolutionary history, being strongest and most aggressive meant being on top of the heap. Although alpha-status has (thankfully) become a bit more nuanced over the past 10,000 years or so, a well-cut jacket that emphasizes your shoulder-to-hip ratio will still appeal to her baser, lustier instincts[1]. This is also a compelling reason for cutting down on beer and junk food and making push-ups part of your daily routine.

Women You can also benefit from the time we spent adapting on the African savannah by wearing clothes that accentuate a small waist in relation to your hip circumference. You might send him running for the door if you verbalize your suitability for child-bearing on the first date, but by emphasizing outward signs of your fertility with your clothing, you're

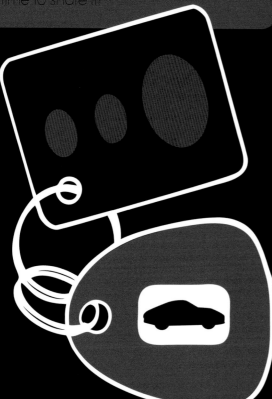

appealing to the vestigial part of his brain that's subconsciously sizing you up for propagating his genes.

"To get him thinking about **kissing you**, look at his mouth occasionally, or subtly touch your tongue to your lips now and then"

Guys Many studies have shown that women react favorably to high-status individuals. You don't need to tell her how much you can bench or hand her last year's tax return to get her interested. Instead, let your body do the talking.

When you walk into a room, take measured, confident steps and minimize superfluous movements. You're giving the impression that you're confident and at ease in the environment. A straight back and slightly elevated chin signal pride, which, according to a 2011 study from the University of British Columbia, is the expression that female test subjects reacted to most positively[2].

Take up some space by standing with your feet slightly apart and your arms open. If you're sitting down, place some personal effects on the table to mark out some territory. By doing so you're displaying that you're confident, competent, and assertive. She, the science suggests, is hard-wired to like that.

Women While the UBC study showed that women react most positively to exhibitions of male pride, it also demonstrated that men find happiness the most appealing expression in women[3]. Smiling and laughing at some of his funnier witticisms, then, may play a role in whetting his appetite. Share some of your own amusing stories, too. Have fun!

You can also show confidence and radiant exuberance by employing more expansive gesticulations. Be your most vivacious self,

"Despite being a bit nervous I tried to be at ease and display confidence, which she seemed to like. That made me feel **more confident**"

enjoy flirting with him wholeheartedly, and advertise the fact that, above all else, you are fun to be around.

If you like, you can signal that he's barking up the right tree by straightening your clothing or touching your hair. Preening gestures indicate interest.

Guys Be casually attentive to her needs. Keep an eye on whether her drink could use freshening up. If she's looking chilly as you head from stop to stop, don't be shy about offering her your jacket. Chivalry may be ailing but it's not quite dead yet and it will be appreciated, I (Grant) can guarantee it. At the risk of sounding like even more of a traditionalist, I do have to say that the onus is still on you to at least offer to pay for drinks, dinner, cab fare, etc. on an early date. If she insists on paying, splitting or picking up the next bill, however, honor her wishes and gracefully accept with a minimum of fuss. This is the 21st century, after all.

My *place?*

Making a smooth transition from bar to bedroom You're at a bar or party, engrossed in a sexually charged conversation with someone extremely alluring— perhaps it's a first or early date, or you've just met. At this point, exchanging numbers or planning another date is skirting the issue. You want sex expeditiously, and early indications are that the gorgeous specimen before you does, too.

There comes a time on every successful precoital date when you're wondering how to float the idea of sneaking off to your place without coming off as presumptuous, or— heaven forbid—creepy. The following tips will help ease the transition from bar to bedroom without too much hand-wringing.

Do your due diligence Through a series of

seemingly casual and conversational questions, deduce whether the prospect of an X-rated sleepover is desirable, or even a practical possibility, for the object of your lust. Ask him or her something like "What are you up to for the rest of the weekend?" If they rattle off a laundry list of commitments, or mention having to get up bright and early (what are they—farmers?), an evening of carnal delight might not be in the cards. If they are, indeed, thinking about shucking you out of your jeans in the immediate future, they'll start hinting at their availability. They might offer a tidbit like "I'm meeting friends for brunch, but nothing before that." No green light, of course, but a tantalizing bit of intel like that can help steel your nerves for the next step.

Establish the geography Over the course

of this or previous chats, you've ascertained where this beautiful creature lives. You're in luck if your place is comparatively close to your present coordinates as you can use this

"You should come back and see my... [insert thing that piqued their interest earlier in the conversation]." **FAIL!**

proximity to your advantage. Don't explicitly say that you live "just around the corner, wink, wink" when you can more suavely mention how the area is changing or otherwise exhibit a local's knowledge of nearby places to eat or things to do. By hinting at how quick and simple it would be to get down to it, you're obliterating potential obstacles to fun in his or her mind.

Give it to them straight There's a lot of

cockamamie advice spewed out by so-called pick-up artists (or PUAs) on the Internet suggesting that it's okay to lure people back to your place for some supposedly practical purpose. These canned lines include gems such as "I'm redecorating my apartment and I'd love to get your opinion on what to do in there" or "You should come back and see my... [insert thing that relates to something that piqued their interest earlier in the conversation]." FAIL! Treat the other person like an adult and your forthrightness will pay dividends. If you've been having a great, flirty chat, there's absolutely nothing wrong with saying simply, "Do you want to get out of here?"

Not only will this get things rolling, but by being a man or woman with a plan you'll also signal your assertiveness, which, as it happens, is sexy (see Call the sexual shots, pp.28–29).

Don't dillydally Nothing will diffuse the sexual tension more than waiting for a bus in a persistent drizzle. Unless your place is a very short walk away, go the extra mile and jump in a cab pronto. You'll be speeding toward sexual nirvana in a semiprivate environment in which you can get a jump start on the kissing and maybe even get your hands on their unmentionables. Have a few denominations of bills at the ready so you don't have to mess around with change and can seamlessly segue into getting him or her inside.

If you've been having a great **flirty chat**, there's nothing wrong with saying simply, "*Do you want to get out of here?*"

Prepare the lair Tips for preparing your bedroom for sex are covered on pp.68–69, but there are things you can do elsewhere at home to grease the wheels of passion. If someone's coming over ostensibly for sex, they're probably not going to don white gloves and run their fingers over the tops of your picture frames. That said, you'd do well to incorporate a bit of tidying up into your getting-ready routine. Don't have dirty dishes in the sink or gym socks on the floor. And, of course, clean the toilet. It's considerate to have fresh towels handy, should they want to take a shower. Have music ready to go (see pp.78–79) and a couple of beers and a bottle of white wine in the fridge. Red can stain the lips—a nitpicky point, perhaps, but it's this sort of attention to detail that will pay off in the end.

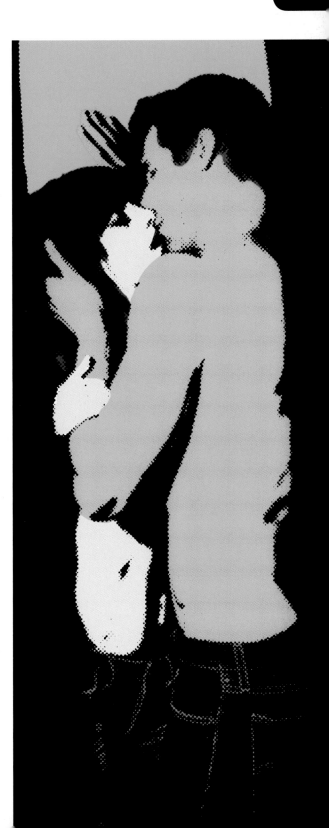

Or *yours?*

Secure yourself a sexy invitation A home advantage is of vital importance if you're, say, a football team—but you're not, so there's no reason to let the prospect of unfamiliar surroundings throw you off your game. An away game frees you up from fretting about whether you remembered to take out the trash or clean the toilet, so you can just relax and enjoy...

Playing away can be very exciting. Beyond the thrill of having sex with a new person in a new venue, there's the added exhilaration of negotiating a strange neighborhood the following morning, enjoying an Americano in a previously unvisited outlet of your preferred coffee chain, replaying last night's events in your head, trying to be inconspicuous about grinning to yourself as you try to figure out how to get home. Ah, life is good! So how do you prepare for a tour of booty?

Be prepared Even though you shouldn't have expectations of being invited to someone's inner sanctum, it's good practice to be prepared if you do get an invite. This could be as simple as ensuring you have a few condoms in your pocket or purse when you head out for the night, or as involved as keeping a change of clothes and a toothbrush at your workplace, should you need to clock in the next morning. A little forethought will mean that your fun, sexual health, or work status won't have to be compromised because you've had an X-rated sleepover.

Point in their direction If your place is too far away, or your housemate is hosting a poker night, use these as reasons why you're not already dragging him or her home. You could say something like "I'd suggest we go back for a drink at my place but it's like a disaster area

Beyond the *thrill of having sex with a new person* is the exhilaration of **negotiating a strange neighborhood**

right now." Now that you've floated the idea of moving on to a private setting, it's not such a big deal for them to suggest their place as an alternative venue.

Be open-minded Being on home turf means that you're more likely to set the sexual agenda. Conversely, if you're playing away, you're more subject to what they like. Their music, their handcuffs, their toys, etc. Playing away, then, can mean exercising some open-mindedness and relinquishing a bit of control. That's a good

GRANT'S SEXPLOITS I once hooked up with a girl who was aghast that I wasn't putting on my pants shortly after we were done. I didn't pick up on it at the time and heard second-hand that she was hoping I'd hit the road promptly after the act. Similarly, I've hosted people and, as they snored away blissfully, found myself thinking that I really should have dropped stronger hints about quitting while we were ahead.

thing. Going with their flow can be a great way to discover things that you incorporate into your own sex menu going forward. I (Grant) once hooked up with a girl who, after sex, cleaned me up with a hot towel (like the ones you're handed when you sit down at a sushi restaurant). It was a relatively simple touch that left a great impression and led me to adopt it myself. (It goes over fantastically well, incidentally.)

Don't impose After you've had sex, gauge the mood at this stage—there's nothing worse than a guest who overstays their welcome. Ask your host if they'd prefer you to leave. You could offer something like "If you need to get up early, I'm totally fine with jumping in a cab." They'll appreciate this courtesy and, more often than not, will invite you to stay—at least until the rooster crows. If, however, they would prefer to sleep alone, don't take it to heart. For a lot of

Playing away can mean exercising *open-mindedness* and *relinquishing a bit of control*. **That's a good thing.**

people, a sleepover can be even more intimate than the sex preceding it. I (Grant) can be a sore-headed, foul-breathed beast in the morning, so cutting out early before the scene is fully illuminated by glaring sunlight can be a good thing. Either way, as their guest, it's up to you to gracefully give them an opportunity to call it a night.

Be a good guest Just because you've been up all night, engaged in activities that are deemed illegal in many states, you are not excused from the responsibility of being a good houseguest. In fact, how considerate you are should be directly proportional to how filthy you got the night before, in our opinion. With that in mind, offer to go and fetch some coffee and doughnuts when you've sated yourselves after a morning session. Don't leave a mess, and offer to help tidy up after you both. Even if this liaison is destined to be a one-night engagement only, there's absolutely no need to smash a hole in the door in your attempt to flee. By showing that you're a considerate grown-up, you're mitigating any awkward moments in the future when you almost inevitably run into one another again. Leave a good impression.

Wrapping up *in bed*

It's the only way The condom is one of the most critical components of being great in bed—especially in the early stages of sex, love, and lust. After all, if either one of you is worried about getting knocked up or winding up with an STI, sex will be far less fun, more inhibited, and will end with you wondering when you can get tested rather than when you can get together again.

Given how important condoms are to safe sex, it's no wonder that phrases such as "No glove, no love" have come into popular use.

Unfortunately, once people move past their teens and early 20s, they become decidedly less smart about condom use. Data from the 2009 *National Survey of Sexual Health and Behavior* (a study of the sex lives of Americans aged 14–94) found that condom use greatly declines with age, and not just because the people who took part in the study had found someone to settle down with[1]. Only about half of men in their 20s and 30s who had recently had vaginal sex with a casual partner said that they had used a condom.

The numbers are even more dismal among the women, with only about 40 percent in their 20s, and 30 percent in their 30s, saying that condoms were a regular part of their casual encounters. In a world full of absentee baby-daddies and HIV and other STIs, not using a condom does not make for a lustful night of sex, let alone a comfortable morning after.

Allow for a choice So how do you have safe sex and phenomenal sex at the same time, without making it an awkward affair? Simple. Bring out your smart-sex kit, then relax and let things flow (so to speak). Following our earlier advice, you have a variety of condoms around

Bonus points if you have a never-been-opened *vibrating condom ring* in that nightstand drawer

YOUR ALL-IMPORTANT PRESEX CONDOM CHECK:

Condoms on hand? Check. Because you've prechecked the expiration dates, you won't even have to turn on the bright lights to look.

Ask your partner if she or he has a condom preference. It's only polite.

Open the packet carefully—this isn't the time to tear it open with one's teeth, as that makes one look more like a damn fool than a sexy beast.

Women: Offer to do the honors when it comes to donning the condom. This gives him more mental space to soak in the arousing aspects of sex (breasts, kissing, hands sliding down his penis), which can help keep his erection strong, throbbing, and focused on you.

Ensure the condom is unrolled to the base of the penis, has no air bubbles trapped in it, and feels comfortable enough to proceed with pleasure.

Now for the lube. The more comfortable you feel with rubbing a dab or two up and down his condom-clad shaft, the better. Although it can also be hot to watch a guy prepare to plunder.

and easily within reach. If you're a man, you've previously tried various condom types and have a clear favorite, but you're chivalrous and smart enough to have other kinds available, including nonlatex condoms, in case he or she is allergic. Bonus points if you have a disposable, never-been-opened vibrating condom ring in your nightstand drawer. If you're a woman, you're equally well-prepared, having made use of a discreet compartment in your handbag.

As for lube, both men and women should have a good supply of water-based lubricant on hand, or at the very least a small single-use pack of lube in their pocket or handbag. If you think there's no room, think again: If there's space enough for a smart phone, there's space enough for smart sex.

If either of you is **worried about getting knocked up** or **winding up with an STI**, sex will be *far less fun*

Low-level awareness Once sex begins, one must maintain some degree of low-level awareness of the condom. It's a buzz kill to think about condoms for every second, and not necessary, anyway. But men should have some sense of how it feels on their penis, which is why choosing a condom that has a noticeable feel to it around the base can be a good reminder that it's on securely. And women may want to check the condom for tears if they feel slight irritation at the point of ejaculation—sometimes a clear sign that semen has leaked out and had contact with the vagina or anus.

The vast majority of times, though, the condom will stay on from beginning to end. And you should keep it on from beginning to end if you want the best chances of reducing pregnancy or STI risk—none of this "just the tip for five minutes" nonsense, or taking it off midway. For the best sex, use condoms consistently until you're certain about each other's STI and HIV status, monogamous, and comfortable with the possibility of becoming parents together.

Get naked *in style*

Never trip over your pants, stockings, jeans again Getting naked in style starts with how you get dressed. The simpler the choices you make when putting clothes on, the easier time you both will have when it's time for your clothes to come off— especially after a glass or two of wine. With a few well-picked items of clothing, and these tips on how best to remove them, you'll never make a fool of yourself again.

What not to wear Women will do best to leave their shapewear (girdles or other constricting undergarments) in their dresser drawer on date night. Not only can removing these items have the appearance of being in a wrestling match with oneself—the seams on too-tight stockings or girdles can leave red marks on the tummy or thighs, triggering feelings of self-consciousness. That's not to say your partner cares, but it doesn't help things along. Plus, sexual arousal and orgasm are eased by feeling relaxed, not by feeling pushed, prodded, or otherwise being tortured into being a size smaller than one is. Love your body, treat it kindly, and wear clothes that fit you comfortably while still looking sexy.

Now that we've established what to avoid, let's talk about what to wear: Choose a top or dress that lifts easily over your head or, better yet, one that unbuttons or unzips so you can easily step out of it. That way you don't need to worry about snagging an earring or messing up your hair—just yet (that comes soon enough). Ask your partner to unhook your bra unless you want to keep it—and your panties—on for a while.

How he gets naked Men generally wear less constricting clothes to begin with, which makes getting undressed easier overall. There are exceptions, though. Trying to remove too-tight jeans can lead to an awkward shimmy,

In *the heat of the moment* you may end up the guy who's leaping into bed **wearing nothing but his socks**

hopping around the room like a bunny—or, worse, tripping and knocking over a lamp or a candle. Choose pants or jeans you can unbutton, unzip, and step out of in a flash.

When it comes to belts, choose one that can be easily undone by a partner who wants to use her hands or her teeth. This isn't a time for sailor-knot belts.

One of men's biggest getting-naked challenges is making sure that, once their pants are off, their underwear isn't a total turn-off. On date night, forget the tighty-whities. And it most certainly is not the night for underwear with holes or that looks dirty in any way. At the very least, underwear—whether boxers or briefs—should fit well and be clean. If you want to get particularly sexy, take a cue from gay men who have been strutting around for decades in underwear that sculpts their butts and packages in the most alluring ways. Brands to look for include H&M, Paul Smith, Diesel, and Bjorn Borg. Good underwear may make your partner salivate with an eagerness to get them off. Also, they're the last thing seen before you get naked, so make a good impression. And don't forget the small but important details: Men may find it easiest to remove their socks around the time their pants come off. Otherwise, in the heat of the moment, they may forget and wind up being the guy who's leaping into bed wearing nothing but his socks.

Take it slow Now a word about timing. Sex doesn't need to be rushed, and taking clothes off one jaw-dropping piece at a time can be incredibly seductive. There's a delicious wait-and-see element to dropping one's handbag to the ground, unbuttoning only one or two shirt buttons, kissing each other's necks and chests, and sliding hands beneath shirts or pants, which just cannot be re-created in hurried stripping. (That can be hot, too, but in a different, feverish kind of way.)

All too often, couples who have been together for years get into a "get naked and get in bed" routine that takes all of 10 seconds. Try to stretch it out, letting one piece of clothing go at a time between long minutes of kissing and caressing. Taking your time—at least 10 or 15 minutes from first kiss to first penetration—can make it easier for women to lubricate and for men to develop a firm erection, and will also prolong the passion.

Removing each other's clothes can be an integral part of the sexual experience rather than only the preamble if you incorporate kissing, touching, and the seductive element of waiting into it. If you do stumble or get stuck on a zipper, try to laugh it off rather than letting embarrassment or frustration wash over you. Sex is a lot of things, including clumsy at times, and that can be part of the fun.

Trying to remove ***too-tight jeans*** can lead to **hopping around the room** like a bunny, or to tripping

Call the *sexual shots*

How to be lady of the house/lord of the manor Confidence and assertiveness are extremely sexy traits in both men and women. Girls, don't let traditional gender roles cause you to hesitate if you feel like driving the bus—men love it when women take the lead. Whether you are male or female, you can signal your assertiveness by being the one who introduces the idea of getting naked.

Take control If you're on a hot date, feeling bold, and have done your due diligence, you can kiss—or even goose—the object of your desire, side-stepping the need to verbalize your intentions. When it's finally go-time, grab your crush by the hand or, if you're feeling theatrical, by the tie or scarf, leading him or her to a place where you can work your magic.

When you're getting down to it, take charge of getting him or her undressed or deny them access to unzipping you. Now you can revel in the power of having your gorgeous partner naked while you're mostly fully clothed.

By taking charge, you're assuming some responsibility for having sex the way you like it and, if your partner is not complaining, the way she or he likes it, too.

> "He went for my zipper, but I took his hand and **held it firmly** behind his back, and I could feel **his heartbeat quicken**"

Delaying gratification Making yourself wait is another way of taking charge. If you know that you enjoy sex more if it's preceded by at least 10 minutes of kissing, grab his or her hands in your own and dictate the pace (see Pronto, or take it slow? pp.112–113). A friend of mine (Grant's) recently complained that a guy she had slept with rushed to get to third base, making it that much harder for her to reach orgasm when they eventually had sex. If she had taken control she could have slowed things down to a pace that works for her. It's worth noting that many guys tend to develop harder, fuller erections if there's more ramping up before the big event, so pull in the reins and make things last.

Power games Clothed female, naked male (CFNM) and clothed male, naked female (CMNF) are both popular kinks and porn subgenres that address the feelings of vulnerability and power involved in this dynamic.

Taking charge If you like being dominant and your partner reacts, don't be shy—give some orders and manipulate them into positions you like (see also Asking nicely, pp.104–105, and Asking nastily, pp.106–107).

Research has found that, contrary to stereotypes, touching, kissing, and cuddling are among the biggest predictors of men's sexual satisfaction[1]. It helps them feel attractive, loved, and, importantly, wanted. So don't hang back—show him what you think of him.

"When I *stroke, kiss, caress, and cuddle him,* he loves it so much I think he's going to start *purring!*"

she thinks...

Women can be complacent.
Given how much we're hit on from adolescence to adulthood, it's too easy to think men are happy just to be invited to the party. All you have to do is show you're game for sex, right? Wrong. Men are sexual human beings, too. Like us, they need to feel attractive and desired. It's a big mistake to think he'll be grateful for even the crumbs you throw his way.

It's true that, while some men are just happy that you're interested, if you want to work toward unusually rich pleasure for the both of you, then get in the habit of expressing your desires. Initiate sex. Take him by the arm or the tie and see if you can kiss your way to the bedroom.

"I think I got as much of a buzz out of *seducing him* as he did"

"In the movie line, I whispered in his ear what I was *planning to do to him later.* I loved the look of *crazed excitement* in his eyes as he tried to act normal"

If you've been together a while, be direct—put your hand between his legs when watching a movie at home. Or, better still, switch off the TV, sit on his lap, and grind against him with your clothes on for a good half hour before making love right there.

"I've snatched **sexual defeat** *from the jaws of victory on* **too many occasions** *to count*"

My blooper reel of date fiascos includes premature kisses, in which my eagerness to make out with a girl eclipsed an accurate reading of the situation, and misreadings of blatant come-ons, leading to wasted opportunities and several women wondering about my sexual orientation.

If you tend to mess things up at the last minute, take a step back and adopt a more laissez-faire attitude to your mode of seduction. You'll still want to have sex just as much, but if things don't turn out as you hoped, you're prepared to not let it spoil your night.

"*I consciously* **decluttered my mind** *and focused on enjoying the flirty banter*"

he thinks ...

"*It wasn't until we were in the shower that I realized I didn't want to go through with it. I invented some flimsy excuse and came off looking like a* **jackass**"

Don't follow your erection blindly. Use your brain, too, when deciding if the connection is right between you.

With the benefit of hindsight, I see that the most cringeworthy of my last-minute mistakes could have been avoided if I'd paid a little more attention to my own motives and to the signals being given out around me, and a little less to my unflagging erection. These kinds of screw-ups have, thankfully, become fewer and farther apart as I've belatedly matured, become more comfortable with myself, and less competitive with my friends.

Chapter 2
The naked truth

Going down—get to grips with her parts

What's where—in depth Women's parts are complex. With so many parts, myths about them, and women's own preferences on what to do to them, it can be difficult to know where to start. Or you may wonder which parts are the most likely bets in terms of private or partnered pleasure. Wonder no longer! Heed these tips next time you explore all the vulva has to offer. The lady of the house is sure to be pleased.

Vulva "Vulva" refers to the entire masterpiece, from the tippy top triangular Mound of Venus to the perineum (the area between her vaginal entrance and anus). If you've called it vagina your whole life, no worries—most people use these terms interchangeably. Aside from strict scientists, doctors, or vulva activists, most people don't care which term you use, as long as you show both the love and respect they deserve.

Vagina The vaginal canal is the inside part that multitasks as a site for fingering, intercourse, holding tampons, and birthing babies—not, of course, at the same time. It isn't rich with nerve endings compared to the nerve-packed clitoris. However, the vagina is a little richer in nerve endings on its front wall, where many women like finger, penis, and sex-toy play to take place.

The vagina is a fascinating world all its own. When women feel excited and aroused, vaginal lubrication helps make it wet and slippery. Also during sexual arousal, women's vaginas often grow in size (in a good way). They go from being about 3in to 4in (7.5cm to 10cm) long, which is not big enough for many erect penises, to being about 5in to 6in (13cm to 15cm) or more long, thanks to a process called vaginal tenting. Combined, vaginal lubrication and tenting are nature's way of saying "come inside, let's play!"

Mons (Mound of Venus) This is the triangular part of the vulva that one can see if a woman is standing around naked, say, in a changing room or bedroom. Au naturel, nearly all women have hair on their mons, but many choose to groom it in a way that may be influenced by their own preference, a partner's request, or the latest fashion trend.

Clitoris If you ask most people to point out the clitoris, they'll point to (or lightly lick, if one is lucky) the small nubby portion that's above the vagina and generally hangs out under the clitoral hood, protecting it from overstimulation. There's more to the clitoris than meets the eye, however. Two branches of it, known as crura, each extend a few inches into the body. These may be stimulated during intercourse, vibrator play, or even Kegel exercises. There are many ways of stimulating this most wonderful of female parts, and later in the book, we'll ask—

and she might beg—you to try it in some very specific ways.

Lips Women have three sets of lips on their bodies—one on their face (pucker up!) and two on their vulva, the inner lips (labia minora) and outer lips (labia majora). The trouble with the terms "minora" and "majora" is that they suggest that the inner (minora) lips are smaller than the outer lips, and that's not always the case. Women's vaginal lips come in various shapes, sizes, and colors, are rarely symmetrical, but may be an integral part of her pleasure. Some women enjoy including their lips in oral sex play or masturbation through touching, nibbling, or gentle pressure.

Perineum Down at the bottom is the perineum, a part of the vulva that's not on many women's radars until they're pregnant or have given birth. Some women who have had children may be particularly sensitive in this area due to scar tissue, which can be a good thing or a bad thing (so ask if there are any sensitivities).

"*I think I know all about myself, then an unintended stroke or tweak* **sends me over the edge,** *and voila! A new way to stimulate me*"

Tackling *his tackle*

Know his ridge from his raphe

There's good reason for the fact that cultures around the world pay tribute to the penis in phallic monuments, skyscrapers, and fountains. The penis is impressive. No other part of the human body goes through such dramatic and highly noticeable (not to mention delicious) changes during sexual arousal—all while being able to serve a variety of important bodily functions.

Men's parts are extraordinary—and, all too often, undervalued, as if size were the only thing that matters. Penises and balls come in all sorts of different shapes and sizes, and are sensitive to varying sensations. Unfortunately, men's bodies are often treated in a simplistic manner—as though men's sexuality is basically an on/off switch controlled by the penis.

The penis and its neighbors (the scrotum, testes, and perineum) deserve more attention than they tend to get. Like the clitoris, the penis has several parts to it. With a little knowledge, interest, and good will, men's partners can master the mysteries of the penis, resulting in more fulfilling sex for everyone involved.

Head of the penis Chief among the parts of the penis is the head (technically called the glans). This is the most sensitive part. It comes from the same embryonic tissue that, in women, develops into the clitoris. This means that it's nerve-rich and has significant potential for pleasure. On the top of the glans is the urethral opening, from which men urinate or ejaculate—fortunately for us all, not at the same time.

Ridge Around the glans is a ridge, also called the corona or the crown of the man's family jewels. On the underside of the penis is a triangular area where the tissue connects. Called the frenulum, this is a particularly sensitive area for some men. Touching it during partnered masturbation play or gently licking it during oral sex can be enormous fun to explore.

Raphe Along the underside, some men have a line called the raphe that extends downwards and may be more visible down the middle of their scrotum. Some guys describe this line as a seam—and, essentially, that's what it is, as it's where tissues come together when babies are formed. If you're curious to see another raphe on your body, check out the roof of your mouth and you may notice a line running down the middle.

Shaft The shaft of a man's penis is less sensitive than the rest of it, but there's great potential for sexual enjoyment here. The shaft tends to get the most attention during masturbation, hand jobs, and oral sex, too. It's less nerve-rich and quite firm while erect, so it can often be gripped with initiative by an excited partner, or squeezed by her vaginal muscles on the way to orgasm.

Scrotum Hanging out near the base of the man's penis is his scrotum, which houses the testes. The testes rise closer to the body during sexual excitement, and some men enjoy having them played with as part of a hand job or oral sex. Other men find testicular play far too sensitive, so ask before you start twirling them around.

Perineum One of the most heated areas of men's impressive parts is the perineum, the area in between the scrotum and anus (sometimes called the taint). When pressed firmly, this area can provide pleasurable prostate stimulation. This is a great indirect way of stimulating the prostate without actually dipping a finger inside the anus and going for it. Although if he wants a finger in there, by all means, enjoy! You may want to cover your finger up with a lubricated condom or latex glove, just to keep things clean.

Circumcision A final but important note: Many men are uncircumcised and have foreskin that hangs over part or all of the head of the penis. Other men were circumcised as infants or, less often, as adults. One study suggests that women who have been with both circumcised and uncircumcised men found it easier to experience orgasm with men who still had foreskin, perhaps because the foreskin provided more girth or stimulation during intercourse. However, it's such an underresearched area that it's not worth worrying about one way or the other. Women experience orgasm with all sorts of different men who own all sorts of different penises. Men should march forward with confidence and swagger and make the most of what they've got.

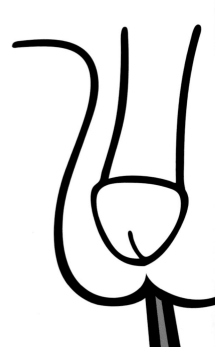

"If I **trim** my pubic hair, my penis looks bigger AND she's more into being down there. How can I lose?"

Sexual *power points*

Plug into the pleasure zones Any part of the human body can be an area of sexual pleasure, seduction, and potentially even of orgasm. However, there are certain areas of both men's and women's bodies that have been found to be particularly ripe for erotic pleasure. Make it your business to know where they are— the payoff is more than worth it.

His spots

F-spot The F in F-spot stands for frenulum, the triangular area at the bottom of the underside of a man's penis glans (head). Try stimulating his F-spot during oral sex by lightly flicking your tongue across it, or gently blowing warm air over the area.

P-spot Men have two P-spots, one external and one internal, with the letter P standing for prostate. The prostate gland is highly sensitive and a source of much pleasure for many—but not all—men, whether they are straight, gay, or bisexual. The prostate gland doesn't really care what a man's sexual orientation is; it just exists and has nerve endings that love attention. Not only is the prostate gland a source of pleasure for many men; it's also a source of fluid. About one-third of the volume of semen comes from the prostate.

To stimulate the external P-spot, press firmly with your fingers or knuckles along the perineum (the area between the scrotum and anus), which is also known as the taint. Some men enjoy touching themselves on the perineum during masturbation, or using a sex toy to target this sensitive area. Others lap up the joys during a hand job, oral sex, or intercourse with a partner. The reverse cowgirl position, in which a woman is on top and facing

The prostate doesn't care what a man's sexual orientation is; it just has *nerve endings that love attention*

her partner's feet, is the ideal position for her to slip two fingers on the taint and press firmly as his arousal builds.

Stimulating the internal P-spot is a much more intimate affair and involves great trust when experienced between two people. So rather than go for this one on the first night, you might do best to wait a while, stimulate the external P-spot and surrounding area, and gauge the lay of the land.

Once you know you're onto a winner, you can slip your lubricated finger inside his anus and use it to stimulate the inner wall of the rectum. Make sure you press the finger toward his penis rather than his rear end. Sex toys such as butt plugs can also be used for inside P-spot play, so ask him what he thinks of them.

Her spots

G-spot Although not given its name until the 1980s, the G-spot has long been known as an area of erotic sensitivity among women. The G in G-spot pays tribute to gynecologist Dr. Ernst Gräfenberg (1881–1957) who, in the 1950s, described the sensual potential of this part of a woman's body.

The G-spot is perhaps best considered a "zone" for stimulating potential rather than a precise spot. Explore her G-spot by gently but firmly using your well-lubricated fingers, penis, or a sex toy to stimulate the front wall of her vagina, penetrating about one to two inches inside the vaginal canal. You can try using a G-spot vibrator, which is curved for focused stimulation. They come in many shapes and sizes, so it might be fun to choose one together. Also, ask her to lie face-down on the bed. In this position, the front wall of the vagina is firmly sandwiched between the bed and your fingers/toy/penis, intensifying the sensations for her.

What's being stimulated during G-spot play? Many scientists believe that the internal parts of the clitoris and/or the erectile tissue that surrounds a woman's urethra may be among the parts that are sensitive to this stimulation.

AFE zone Scientific research on the anterior fornix erogenous (AFE) zone—sometimes called the A-spot—is lacking. Some people suggest that stimulation of this part of the vagina—deep inside the vagina on the front wall—may result in enhanced arousal and vaginal lubrication. Deep fingering or intercourse positions are among the ways in which a couple can explore the AFE zone.

Explore her G-spot using your *fingers, penis, or a sex toy* to stimulate the front wall of her vagina

Consider *your parts*

Genital self-image How we feel about our parts matters a lot. If you don't like them, you won't LOVE sex, so it pays to familiarize yourself with your genitals (if you haven't already)—and to learn to love them. Stare your hang-ups in the face (or mirror) with an open and inquisitive mind and you'll soon see why it is that your partner loves to spend so much time down there.

So it's not as big as a porn star's...

Have you ever considered that she might actually be quite grateful for that?!

A few men have giant penises, and a few men have tiny penises, and the vast majority of men have penises in the average (five-to-seven-inches-when-erect) range. But that fact doesn't keep men from fretting about how they measure up. According to a recent British study, 45 percent of men aren't satisfied with the length or girth of their penis, and an even greater proportion wouldn't say no to an extra inch or two. I (Grant) include myself in this latter grouping (because whipping out a unit that elicited a round of applause would be really, really nice).

Being overly, obsessively concerned with the size of your member, however, is one expression of body dysmorphic disorder, in which you obsess about a perceived physical defect. This psychological disorder is the root cause of anorexia and obsessions such as competitive bodybuilding. So you don't want to go there.

Why is teeny-wiener syndrome so pervasive? It might have something to do with the fact that the only erect penises most heterosexual males ever see are in porn. But remember that porn actors are a self-selecting bunch whose much-larger-than-average penises are a prerequisite for the job. Also, men are usually gazing down at their penises from above, which tends to have a foreshortening effect.

95 percent of men have penises in the average *(five-to-seven-inches-when-erect)* range

The good news is that, because of this foreshortening effect, you've probably got more than you think. The better news is that, generally, men place considerably greater importance on the size of their Johnsons than their partners do. The take-home message is that loving what you've got is going to increase

THE SCIENCE PARTS Several studies from my (Debby's) research team at Indiana University show that how we feel about our genitals matters to sex and health[1]. Women who feel more positively about their parts tend to be more likely to masturbate, to use a vibrator, to have an easier time having an orgasm during oral sex, to have regular gynecological checkups, and to experience better sexual function overall (i.e., **higher desire, arousal, sexual satisfaction, and easier orgasms and vaginal lubrication**). Men who feel more positively about their parts also experience better sexual function, including **better sexual desire, erectile function, sexual satisfaction, and orgasm**.

your enjoyment of sex. Forever longing for a cucumber-sized appendage is definitely going to detract from it.

Girls have hang-ups, too A similar aesthetic standardization in porn has many women feeling sheepish about what's between their legs. There really is a lot of variety in genitals and it's best to celebrate your unique situation, rather than have unnecessary feelings of self-consciousness about what's down there, or even consider taking drastic measures to "correct" perceived imperfections.

Worrying about if you look "ugly" down there *gets in the way* of being able to **let go and experience orgasm**

For many men, getting face-time with a beautiful vulva works like nature's Viagra. Being denied access because a woman feels her muff's not up to snuff is a crying shame.

My (Debby's) scientific research has established that women tend to worry more often than men about their overall appearance. And, unfortunately, worrying if they look "ugly" down there often gets in the way of being able to let go, open themselves to pleasure, and to experience orgasm.

Women can learn to feel sexier about their vulvas by checking them out in the mirror to see what their partners see (and crave). Part by delicious part, check out the clitoris, the inner and outer labia, and the vaginal entrance. Imagine your partner zeroing in on the clitoris, or licking (or even nibbling) the labia. Try seeing your body through his or her hungry, adoring eyes, and you may come to see it in an entirely new light.

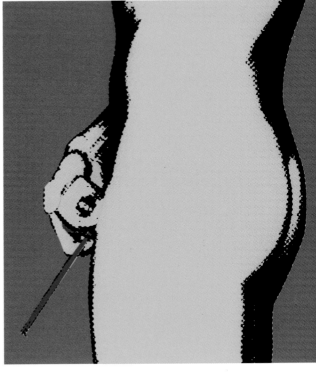

Genital *gym*

Feel the squeeze Like our legs, arms, and abs, our genitals need a good workout to stay in shape. Masturbation and sex help keep them fit (frequent blood flow to the genitals, thanks to arousal, carries oxygen to genital tissue), but sex-savvy women and men would be wise to learn the basics of a good genital workout regimen that's easy to maintain.

Kegel exercises The pelvic floor muscles support orgasmic function as well as urinary continence in both women and men. One of the best ways to keep the pelvic floor muscles toned is by practicing Kegel (kay-gull) exercises. To identify these muscles, stop the flow of urine the next time you're peeing. The same muscles you use to suddenly stop peeing are the muscles that you'll want to work on during Kegel exercises.

Now that you know how to find your pelvic floor muscles, it's time to put them to work. The box on this page contains routines for you to practice. Some women find it helpful to insert a finger into the vagina—if you can feel the finger being squeezed, that's a sign that you're contracting the correct muscles.

Some women enjoy using Ben Wa balls or Kegel exercise "barbells" (special weighted devices that can be used for pelvic floor exercises). If such products are being used inside the vagina, women should take care to use them correctly (check out Debby's book *Read My Lips: A Complete Guide to the Vagina and Vulva* for detailed information) and to clean them properly and carefully before and after use. Such toys should never be inserted into the anus or rectum.

Although it is often recommended that we do pelvic floor exercises daily for optimum benefit, the reality is that many of us forget and

Some women find that *squeezing their pelvic floor muscles* helps them **experience orgasm**

busy ourselves with other types of work, exercise, or social activities. That's okay—just try to find something that might help you incorporate them into your life more often than you do now. Some people set daily alarms to remind them to practice pelvic floor exercises for a few minutes each day. Others try to squeeze in some

PELVIC FLOOR EXERCISE ROUTINES

There are several variations of pelvic floor exercises that you can do. For example, you might:

Hold it Squeeze your pelvic floor muscles for 30 seconds, then release for 10 seconds. Repeat daily for 5 to 10 minutes.

Pulse it Squeeze your pelvic floor muscles for two seconds, then release for two seconds. Repeat daily for two to three minutes.

Slow build Slowly take about 5 to 10 seconds to contract (squeeze) your pelvic floor muscles. Then, slowly release them completely before beginning the cycle again. Repeat daily for 5 to 10 minutes.

squeezes while they wait at traffic lights, when their phone rings, or during otherwise dull weekly staff meetings (it can certainly make them more interesting). The trick is to link the practice of the exercises to a minor regular occurrence in your life, so that each time, say, the telephone rings, it triggers your memory to practice a few quick squeezes.

Sexy squeezes

Pelvic floor exercises can also be done during sex or masturbation. Some women find that squeezing their pelvic floor muscles helps them experience orgasm, alone or with a partner. Men who have sex with women often find it pleasurable to have their partner squeeze her vagina around his penis during sex (which mimics the contractions that lead to her orgasm). Similarly, some men find that practicing pelvic floor exercises can help enhance their erection (and their partner may enjoy feeling

his penis "dance" during slower, more gentle periods of intercourse).

Women who are pregnant or who have recently given birth should ask their healthcare provider if there are certain pelvic floor exercises that he or she recommends doing, as personal healthcare recommendations vary according to your situation. Also, women who experience genital pain or pain during sexual activity should talk to their healthcare provider, or a physical therapist who specializes in genital health, before starting to exercise the pelvic floor muscles. This is because some healthcare providers feel that pelvic floor muscles that are too tight or "overtoned" may contribute to pain. For women who may have overtoned pelvic floor muscles, physical therapists may prescribe exercises to help relax the muscles rather than tone them even more.

Finally, try to enjoy your pelvic floor exercises. Some women and men find them to be an arousing way to stay in top genital shape—and some lucky women even report experiencing orgasm midexercise.

Hedge *trimming*

Pubic topiary—what's hot and what's prickly Given how small the pubic area is, it's astounding that there are so many things one can do with it. Either extreme is a bit of a bold move— and then there's the safety zone of the groomed middle. With changing practices and norms related to pubic hair, many people want to know what to do with the hair down there. Use this guide as you consider your next style.

Retro bush Long sported by men, the retro bush (more lately referred to as the "hipster bush") has been making a comeback among women who are often tired of the pressures— not to mention the razor bumps and high-priced waxing bills—that accompanied the Brazilian rage of the late 1990s and early 2000s.

Retro bush is a bit WYSIWYG—it's a bold move for a first encounter, making it clear that it's your body and you'll do what you like with it, trends be damned. And while it can be a sexy look, be warned that a particularly long retro bush might lower your chances of oral sex among all but the most die-hard muff enthusiasts.

"the **retro bush** makes a statement: I like me just as nature intended"

"to a ⬥ guy, a **heart-shaped bush** can be a romantic gesture"

Trimmed With a trimmed look, the natural hairline is maintained; it's just that scissors or clippers are taken to one's pubic hair to shorten and neaten the hairs. Doing so may help a woman or man maintain as many potentially pheromone-trapping hairs as they can while increasing their odds of having someone's tongue come over to play.

Pruned Consider this as taking the trimmed look to the next level. The natural hairline is a thing of the past as women, more than men, fashion their pubic hair into a design of their or their partner's liking. One of the most common designs is the landing strip, which many associate with porn actresses and exotic dancers, which leaves a thin strip of hair down the center of the mons pubis. Other times, women shave their hair into hearts, stars, or even the first initial of their partner's name.

Bare The bare look became popular among women in the late 1990s and sparked the growth of salons offering Brazilian or "Hollywood" waxes. Long common among gay men, an increasing number of straight men followed their female partners and ditched their hair in the 2000s.

While some doctors note that rates of pubic lice (crabs) have decreased since the advent of the Brazilian, not everyone is convinced that baring all is the way to go. Frequent removers note razor burn from regular and widespread shaving. Waxers note high cost and pain during total waxing as deterrents. And women who are into laser hair removal don't necessarily want to commit to permanent removal in this area in case the trend reverses and they're stuck looking like a prepubescent girl.

Partnered play It's not a style; it's a lifestyle—or at least a sexy lifestyle. Regardless of how you decide to shape (or leave) your pubic hair, why not do it together? Many partners find that sex is that much better when they prep each others' bodies in seductive ways. Some make "shaving" dates (make sure to be completely sober before taking a razor to your partner's parts). Others simply incorporate presex grooming into their foreplay, such as by using a shared bath time to talk about their days (building intimacy), clean up, shave, or otherwise groom, and rub each other's soapy bodies in ways that enhance arousal.

"Shave it, wax it, clip it, let it grow, but remember this: Trends and tastes in how to arrange one's pubic hair are subject to change"

Men are often particularly concerned about their penis size and, less often, the size of their balls. Try to praise his penis without making it seem as if you are doing it as part of your charitable work. No one wants to feel pitied.

> "I have to admit, I wouldn't say no to a couple more inches, but *she says it fits her like a glove*, so I don't feel as though I'm letting her down"

he thinks...

Let him know he's got what it takes to keep you satisfied. Tell him how well his penis fits your body. Not only is the fit great (and orgasmic, as the case may be), but the taste—did you mention how good it tastes? And how much you love to lick it and suck on it? Or massage it with your hand? Squeeze it with your vagina? How it feels when it pushes its way into you? Hearing it helps him to feel good.

If you compliment him, it has to be in earnest—and it has to make sense. If you tell him that he has the biggest penis in the world, 10 seconds on a porn site is all he needs to know that's not true.

> "She said 'mmmm,' so I knew she liked having *her lips around me*—phew!"

> "Sometimes she gets *SO engrossed* in my erection, I think she's forgotten I'm attached to it!"

Remember—actions speak louder than words. Go down on him with a passion. Plow forward with pleasurable, yummy oral sex as if you're in heated competition for the best-penis-licker-on-the-planet trophy.

"*Sometimes, in the middle of going down on me, he looks up at me and tells me I'm gorgeous! Talk about cup runneth over!*"

Men can wholeheartedly express adoration for their partner's parts, both verbally and nonverbally. Licking and eating up with abandon, with a wild, excited look in one's eyes, can make the person who's being pleasured feel beautiful, attractive, and craved.

Guys, let her know how beautiful her vulva is in delicious detail. Her vaginal lips? Gorgeous shades of ever-changing pinks, reds, browns, or whatever shade of wonderment frames her vagina. Her labia are beautifully shaped, like an orchid, seashell, heart, or angel's wings.

"*I love how he licks my clitoris... slowly, and with a lot of love*"

she thinks...

"*I looked in the mirror to try and see what he sees and I began to get what he means. It is beautiful*"

The fact that nearly all natural labia are asymmetrical and vary in color can help women to accept and love these perfectly imperfect parts of their bodies.

A striking paradox among men is that many grew up teasing girls about their vaginas smelling of fish or being "gross." Then, as adults, some take marketing or advertising jobs with companies pushing feminine "hygiene" products onto women. And yet, they throw their hands up in the air, frustrated, when their girlfriends don't want them to go down on them. Would you connect the dots, please?

Shiver *spots*

Private parts aside... what other bits should you stimulate? Given how instrumental the genitals are when it comes to sex, it's not at all difficult to understand why they often steal the show. But being memorably great in bed—whether as a one-night stand or a long-term mate—means attending to all the other delicious parts of a partner's body that make them phenomenally sensual.

Of course, it's not practical to pay homage to each succulent part every time two people get naked. But it is possible—and recommended—to pay more attention to nongenital parts more often. Consider the following information.

During foreplay Try not to dive too quickly to their private parts. Sex isn't a race and no one benefits from getting it on in a rush, as it takes time for penises to fully grow into firm erections, and for vaginas to get as wet as can be. Instead, let your lips linger on your partner's neck and collarbone. Caress their shoulders and back like you're sixteen and unsure how far you can go. And while you're kissing, why not kiss their ears or massage their scalp using the best slow moves you can remember enjoying from your hairdresser.

Once you're naked When the clothes come off, keep up the exploration, particularly with a steady partner you're spending some months,

years, or your entire life with. Think of the bigger picture rather than a particular sex act. Every now and then—say, at least once every 10 or 20 times you have sex with your partner—make an effort to kiss your partner from the tips of their toes all the way up to their lips, skipping over the genitals entirely until later on in your lovemaking. Be bold about turning them over if you crave the side you don't momentarily have access to. With similar frequency, make time for a long, drawn-out, full-body massage or an hour spent carefully bathing each other in a tub big enough for two. Having candles nearby and scented oils in the bathtub can make for a delightful time (the oils can make your touch more slippery, changing the feel and texture of breast touching and other kinds of massage).

Build up to oral sex Before diving in, give some love to your partner's thighs. Tug gently on their pubic hair, if they have any, or run your fingers through it in circles. Many people enjoy being kissed on their thighs and it can be a pleasant surprise if it's been some time.

Many women feel as though they'd like more attention to their breasts during sex with a partner, so make sure to caress her breasts. You might cup them with your hands, massage them in circles, or kiss around them as you circle softly towards her nipples. If she likes more intense stimulation, nibble to the extent she prefers. (If you're not sure, ask first.)

Similarly, many men feel as though their bodies are largely neglected during sex. As such, let your hands explore his body during intercourse. Grabbing his butt can be sexy, as can running your hands up and down his back during missionary. In reverse cowgirl, there's ample opportunity to lean forward toward his legs and kiss them, which also gives him an unparalleled view of where your parts come together.

Keep in mind that sex is bigger than intercourse—that it involves a range of touches, kisses, licks, grabs, sucking, teasing, moans, and even moments of sloppy spit. To the extent that you can mix up sex and include a range of body parts and a variety of techniques in the game—at least from time to time—you'll both be in a better position to keep sex interesting for the night or for the long haul.

"I have **several spots that make me shiver** and it's true to say I gauge new partners by how many of them they find"

"Show initiative in bed by reaching for the **parts you want**, redirecting your partner's hands to a preferred place, or flipping them over into a sexier position. Letting each other know what **feels amazing** can only improve sex for you both."

Putting up *barriers*

Condoms and other contraceptives When it comes to great sex, it can be very tempting to just plunge straight in. But all grown-ups know that, unless you want to risk catching an STI or you actively want a baby, there are no two ways about it—you need to put up barriers or, sooner or later, nature will find a way. Be playful and open-minded and you'll find they can be fun to use—if you know how.

Singles' sex If having babies is not on your to-do list, using contraception definitely is. Then there's the issue of STIs. There are a lot of them out there—chlamydia, HPV, HIV, and gonorrhea, to name just a few. Until you're monogamous and have both been tested for STIs, the best protection you have against STIs and unwanted pregnancies is in the form of the condom.

We're conditioned to think that sex sensations diminish with the use of condoms. Men and women talk about it, comedians joke about it, and sex in porn is almost entirely condom-free. Here's some advice: Whether or not condoms are an action-stopping, passion-killing, erection-deflating drag is entirely up to you. An ever-expanding line of condoms means that there's more choice than ever before, including condoms that are ribbed, studded, have a baggier shaft (that help sex feel more natural), and that come with vibrating rings, as well as performance-enhancing condoms that can help men last a little longer than usual. For those who are latex-sensitive, there's a selection of nonlatex condoms. Find out which brand and style you like best, whether you like to put them on or would enjoy seeing your partner slowly roll

GRANT'S SEXPLOITS Condoms and I didn't get off to a good start. Before I'd even got one on, I was highly aware of the prospect of fiddling clumsily with the packaging, and presumed there would be less sensation. In retrospect, it was hardly surprising that, despite how eager I was to lose my virginity, my penis went soft the moment it was time to wrap up for the first time. Mentally scarring? Just a bit. It took me many years, scores of sexual partners, three bouts of chlamydia, several nerve-racking HIV tests, and a handful of pregnancy scares to figure out that condoms don't have to be a hindrance to fun. One of the biggest turning points for me was when I made wearing a condom a kink, with the help of a girlfriend who was serious about condom use and helped me realize how much fun using them could be. She got me thinking that putting one on was like suiting up for battle, and helped me change my mind-set from "this condom is going to diminish my enjoyment" to "this condom is ultimately going to help me have more worry-free sex."

Bearing in mind that no method is 100 percent reliable, two methods are better than one. Condoms can be overlooked by couples, but are an instrumental part of solid birth control. As mentioned, there is a huge variety available, and they are easy and fun to use. Many couples who do not want to get pregnant will use condoms plus the birth control pill.

Although rumors abound about male birth control, so far no such pill, spray, or shot exists.

> "I think *if condoms were used more in porn,* a lot more guys wouldn't whine so much about using them"

one on, and make them an integral part of your date kit. Whether sex feels better with or without condoms is up to you.

Couples' sex When a couple wants to have a baby, sex becomes a no-holds-barred affair, but for the gazillion times birth control is necessary, there are many methods available.

Birth control technologies have advanced significantly over the past decade and options now include the birth control pill, patch, shot, and ring. The birth control pill remains among the most effective methods of contraception. Only men with extremely good ejaculatory control (i.e., it doesn't just sneak up on them), should ever use withdrawal (pulling out) as a method of birth control, though we advise that it's not worth the risk.

Fun time It's a total misconception that using condoms is a drag. There's lots of fun to be had with them, which is a fact condom manufacturers have not been slow to catch up on, so shop around and use your imagination.

History *herstory*

Friendly ways to share your sexual pasts Hearing graphic descriptions of your partner's previous sexploits is fascinating. These tales can be amusing, arousing, astonishing, abominable, or awe-inspiring, and ultimately they impart an invaluable sense of perspective, not only into your partner's turn-ons and sense of sexual adventure, but also about what goes on out there in the world.

When you and your partner share sex stories, you quickly realize that the seriously naughty thing you like to do really isn't so weird in the greater scheme of things, you become privy to ready-made examples of the kinds of activities that push his or her buttons, and you take some dark pleasure in knowing that there's an incredible number of people who simply don't have a clue what they're doing in bed. (By reading this book, of course, you're ensuring that you won't be one of them.)

If you feel comfortable hearing your partner's sexual history, then get on with it (perhaps not while you're actually having sex, though). While talking about your sex likes and dislikes, take turns sharing your past sexcapades. Looking over each of your pasts, which experience would each of you rate as Most Adventurous Sex? Most Blah? Or the thing that you would try again in a heartbeat if you only had a wiling partner? Or—even better—the thing that you and your ex always dreamed of experimenting with, but never quite had the guts to try...

In summary, swapping sex stories is an enlightening, humanizing dialogue that's well worth having, once you feel comfortable with it.

Getting comfortable with it While it's true
that hearing details of past sexcapades can open doors to new exploration together, as a sex educator and columnist I (Debby) have heard far too many stories of uncomfortable, even angry, conclusions to these conversations. Not everyone is welcoming and secure about their partner's past revelries.

Even for those who are comfortable with the idea of their partner having a colorful past, certain stories can trigger feelings of jealousy, especially if they involve a previous partner or experience that's difficult to compete with. When I (Grant) first heard that my girlfriend's ex-boyfriend was known throughout the greater Melbourne area for his boa constrictor–like schlong, I almost threw up on the spot. This man was implored to whip it out at parties! He would display it at bars in exchange for free drinks! But then, as my girlfriend and I talked, she revealed that performing oral sex on him was challenging, that a number of her favorite sexual positions were uncomfortable, that anal sex was... ahem... a pipe dream, and that having intercourse for more than 10 minutes resulted in her suffering from a painful urinary tract infection. They just weren't the best fit for each other. Good sex is predicated on both parties being a good fit, both figuratively and literally. It's worth listening from this perspective as you hear tales that have the potential to bring out the green-eyed monster in you.

This story shows that it can be worth getting into a dialogue about previous experiences that could be tricky, but might end up leading to sexy exchanges that ultimately enhance one's relationship. So what to do? Tread carefully. If your partner wants to know—or if you do—talk about your curiosities first. How secure do both of you feel about sharing stories? Have you had similar conversations with exes in the past? How did they go? Also, it's a good idea to start small—don't, for example, begin by sharing stories about the best sex you've ever had, lest one or both of you feel insecure or jealous. Why

Keep the **lines of communication open** with a view to keeping sex *exciting, satisfying, and fun*

not start by sharing a story about the first time or an embarrassing or awkward time that you had sex? And, by all means, try to tame your story a little, just to make sure everyone walks away feeling as if they can be on par with their partner's past.

To increase the odds of your story sharing going over well, you might add a detail about what you wish had gone differently, or what you'd like to try differently—with your current partner, in the here and now or coming weeks/months. That way, the past is used only as an example, but your focus is on your future and the person lying in bed with you.

Reserve judgment Even people who are too squeamish to hear details of their partner's previous adventures will often try to extract or deduce an estimate of the notches on their bedpost. (It's worth remembering here that men and women tend to fudge the numbers when asked outright. Men tend to egregiously exaggerate[1].) Whether your partner's previous conquests could comfortably fit in a Mini Cooper or fill an entire stand at a football stadium, accept their history. If he or she is having a great time in bed with you, the people in his or her past are probably not at the forefront of his or her mind. The onus, then, is on you, dear reader, to keep the lines of communication open with a view to keeping sex exciting, satisfying, and fun.

Chapter 3
Me, myself, and I

Why me-time *is good*

The benefits of self-love Not only has masturbation been shown to be completely harmless to your physical and emotional wellbeing; there's a very strong case for the idea that it's good for you, not to mention that it makes you a better sex partner. On a fundamental level, masturbation is training for sex, and we would venture that some of the world's best lovers were at one time prodigious pullers and relentless rubbers.

Luckily, we live in an age in which masturbation is regarded as perfectly normal—at least in the civilized world. Just over 100 years ago, however, it was a different story. "Neither the plague, nor war, nor small-pox, nor similar diseases, have produced results so disastrous to humanity as the pernicious habit of Onanism," said a Dr. Adam Clarke, prompting Dr. John Harvey Kellogg—yes, the guy who invented Corn Flakes—to recommend unspeakable barbarisms such as sewing boys' foreskins shut and burning off young girls' clitorises with acid. Luckily, these draconian measures didn't catch on, although medical circumcision of infants became standard procedure in North America (and, to a lesser extent, Australia, New Zealand, South Africa, and the UK) as a not-particularly-effective hedge against boys and men fecklessly jerkin' the gherkin.

Nowadays, thankfully, we are more enlightened about sex in general, and modern wisdom advises that teenage boys and girls be left in peace and privacy to find out all about their parts.

Training for sex People who are on familiar terms with their genitals have a pretty good idea of what they like and don't like. Having that knowledge means that they can finagle almost any situation to their liking by gently giving guidance and avoiding listless fumblings and a

People who are on *familiar terms with their genitals* have a pretty good idea of **what they like and don't like**

severely chafed penis/vagina. This treasure trove of intimate know-how can only be gathered over countless hours clocked up getting to know yourself.

Masturbation teaches you how to make yourself feel good, but it also hones your senses so that you know when things are feeling a little too good, a little too quickly. We're talking, of course, about knowing your own sexual response. Guys: If you're teetering at the point of no return, a strong background in "Onanism" will mean that you'll know when to stop the

HEALTHY BONUS Masturbation is not just good—it's good for you. Studies have shown that **men who ejaculate more often are lowering their risk of getting prostate cancer[1]**. Frequent ejaculation has also been linked to lower blood pressure, better cardiovascular health, and it is an enjoyable way of keeping depression at bay. In 2009, a leaflet was issued in Britain carrying the slogan "An orgasm a day keeps the doctor away[2]!"

stimulation and cool off for a bit before resuming (see Cool Your Jets, page 160). If you really do your homework, you can get to the point where you can practically come on command, which is handy. Women: Knowing that an orgasm is imminent will mean that you can firmly tell your partner not to stop under any circumstances.

Just for fun Of course, masturbation is a perfectly acceptable pastime, even if you're not in training for sex. It's free, it sends a rush of

If you're not feeling as sexual as usual, _a little me-time_ might be just the tonic to get you **firing on all cylinders**

happy-making endorphins around your body, it can help you nod off to sleep after a stressful day, and, you know, it's right there!

Almost everybody goes through periods in which they're not feeling very sexual. That's fine for a while but if you feel as if something's missing in your life, having a little me-time might be just the tonic you need to get firing on all cylinders again. Later on in the book we suggest that premeditated sex can be the antithesis of sexy, but this doesn't apply when you're planning on getting lucky with yourself. Put a little time into your festival of narcissism and set aside a luxurious evening in which to diddle. Aggregate your favorite porn, purchase a recommended lube, lock your bedroom door, and indulge yourself, experimenting with the hand-jive techniques discussed in the following chapters.

Jacking *off*

Different strokes I (Grant) literally can't remember a time before I was an avid masturbator. However, until I was around thirteen, I didn't so much jerk off as hump carpeted flooring. But at a certain age, I decided that hitting the deck to siphon off some off my young lust was impractical and, with difficulty, weaned myself away from it—getting through an extraordinary amount of hair conditioner in the process.

The point is, even if you've been palming yourself off efficiently for ages, it's important to remain open to change. You never know—you might find something that you consider a huge improvement. Here are a few tips to spice up your Onanism.

Habit of a lifetime Think about how you usually do it, then do the opposite. Do you do your pulling when you are lying on your back? Try it lying on your front, standing up, sitting or kneeling. Do you regularly watch porn as you masturbate? Try going old school and run through some of your most exciting fantasies or the highlight reel of some of your most gratifying sexploits. By regularly changing things up, you're helping to ensure that you won't condition yourself to one particular set of stimuli. Not only is this variety going to introduce you to exciting new sensations, it's going to come in very handy when you're getting down with a partner.

Singlehanded The most common masturbation technique—and the basis of a well-known offensive hand gesture—is when the four fingers are curled around the penis, with the thumb curling around the top to meet them. You can start to mix things up from this standard position. First straighten your middle, ring, and pinkie fingers so that you're giving the okay hand gesture. You might find the concentrated pressure in this ring a novel sensation. If you're a no-lube guy, give some slip 'n' slide a whirl. You might find that lubricant takes your standard wanking technique to a whole new level. Flip your grip and try an overhand maneuver so that your thumb is closest to your body and pinkie is farthest away, like you're throwing dice at a craps table. This should change the sensation and alter your stroke rhythm. While trying these variations, with your free hand cup your plums or gently pull them away from your body or apply pressure to your perineum and massage it in a small circular motion.

Two-handed Get ambidextrous and awaken yourself to twice the possibilities. Interlink your fingers like you're about to pass a volleyball. Then insert your penis in the entrance to your hand cave—lube would definitely be a good thing here. You can either move your hands up and down the shaft or keep them in one place and move your hips to more closely replicate sex. Either way, the head of your penis will peek out from where your index fingers and thumbs are making a circle. Feeling pressure from both of your palms should feel very different from the typical one-handed style. Without too much muscle power, you should be able to make it extra snug in there. Alternatively, you can clutch the base of your penis with your left hand and the top half with the right. Sort of a one potato, two potato thing. From here you can ensconce your entire penis with your touch or, if you've got the lube handy, try gently twisting your wrists like you're giving your pecker a slippery "Indian burn." If it actually feels like burning, stop for goodness sake! Another two-fisted favorite of mine is a slippery hand-over-hand motion like you're letting out a length of rope.

"Trying new techniques on my own has made me more relaxed with a partner—it's win-win"

Smooth operator Sharing a room with friends has taught me that you can get yourself off with hardly any telltale movement at all. Try gripping your cock in the standard way, then circling a thumb over the ridge (corona) of the head of your penis. You can also do the same thing around the front to your banjo string (frenulum). Experiment with tiny motions until you happen upon something that you really like. No one ever needs to know what you're up to and the long haul flights will be a lot less boring—provided you have a blanket.

Look, no hands! Go back to my old standby and hump something. Put a towel down or even wear a condom to make cleanup easy and start wanking in a way that's closer to actually having sex.

Jilling *off*

Hit it, sister Female masturbation is much less talked about than its male counterpart, but this doesn't mean it is any less acceptable, enjoyable, or fun. Whether enjoyed as the main sexual event or as a tasty side, most women find it a great way of getting to know their bodies and sexual preferences—which, in turn, can only improve sex with a partner. In short, there is nothing to lose and everything to gain.

Growing up, the first time I (Debby) stumbled across the term "masturbation" was in a women's magazine that I was probably too young to be reading at the time. Interestingly, the author actually defined the term, indicating that masturbation could involve touching a variety of one's own body parts in ways that felt good, including the genitals, breasts, thighs, and so on. In other words: I was fortunately exposed, early on, to the idea that self-pleasuring wasn't a down-there-only kind of experience. Not only was this a helpful lesson as a young woman, but it turned out to be a helpful reminder in my work as a scientist who studies sex. After all, if you ask people only what they do with their penises and vaginas, you miss a whole lot of wonderful ways that masturbation plays out in people's lives.

Taboo, schmaboo Women's sexuality is still considered more taboo to discuss openly compared to men's sexuality. Also, the ways in which people talk about young women and sex are often more about being "careful" and "safe" or about women "putting on the brakes" rather than enjoying and initiating sex. There's a "boys will be boys" mentality when it comes to men—and even young boys—and masturbation. And there's long been an uncomfortable silence when it comes to conversations about women and masturbation. Fortunately, much of that has been changing in recent decades.

And yet, just because people rarely talk about female masturbation doesn't mean that it doesn't exist. Women who are asked to recall their early masturbation frequently tell stories of immense pleasure that they experienced while riding in a bumpy car, doing sit-ups, taking a bath, sitting on a washing machine, touching themselves, sliding against their bed or pillows, "borrowing" their mother's back massager, or wearing tight jeans.

Thinking about this diversity in young women's early sexual experiences can help make for better masturbation as an adult. So next time you find yourself with some time on your hands, why not give some of the following ideas a go?

Try a vibrator According to a study that our research team conducted, 46 percent of US women ages 18 to 60 had used a vibrator during masturbation alone. Choose one that feels right to you. If you generally experience pleasure or orgasm from vaginal penetration, you might want one that can be inserted into the vagina. If you're more into clitoral stimulation, then an external vibrator may be a good choice for you.

Vary your wetness As a woman, you may be used to feeling that you have to work with what you've got in terms of vaginal wetness. And yet many women find that lubricant ups the ante when it comes to their masturbation. In a study that involved 2,453 lubricant-using women, we found that women mostly used lubricant for reasons of fun and pleasure rather than trying to solve a problem (such as discomfort or insufficient vaginal lubrication). Try water-based lubricant one time and the longer-lasting silicone-based another (unless you're using silicone sex toys—then stick with water-based lubricant). Use a pea-sized dab one day and a big dollop the next, just to see how it feels.

Change positions Just as couples sometimes get stuck in a sex position rut, individuals can find themselves sticking to their same old masturbation routine. Some women lie back as if they're in missionary while they pleasure themselves with their fingers or a sex toy. Others lie face down on their bed while sliding their

bodies against pillows. Keep in mind that these are only two of many sumptuous possibilities. One can attach a dildo with a suction cup to a door or wall and back oneself up to it. Or straddle a dildo placed in between cushions (in addition to fun masturbation, this is great practice for woman-on-top positions with a partner).

Make it a whole body experience
Remember that early definition of masturbation that I once read? Don't leave your other body parts out of the fun. A little massage lotion on your breasts can make for some slippery-good self-touching. Squeezing your pelvic floor muscles can alter the way masturbation feels. Changing what you think about can enhance masturbation, too—whether conjuring up images from your own sexual experiences, novels, movies, lingerie catalogs, or porn. It's your masturbation—make the most of it.

"I love to experiment with what *feels good*. It's like having a partner focused entirely on me"

Tools of the manual trade

Preparation: lube, tissues, erotica, nail file... Masturbation is like frozen lasagna with dual cooking instructions—the quick microwave version and the much slower oven-cook method. Everyone knows that using the oven will likely result in better heating (no cold insides for you), a more succulent taste, and perhaps even a tasty bit of browning on the edges.

Both sexes tend to agree that masturbation is more fulfilling when there's been enough time for buildup, which can result in a more satisfying and intense release. We are aware that, some nights, you're so hungry, or so rushed for time, that only the quick microwaved lasagna will do. When you do have the time to prepare for a great main course, however, the following suggestions for hotter hand- and finger-play are for you.

Take stock of your supplies Make sure you have everything you need. This may be a charged laptop, fresh porn download or DVD, lubricant, hand lotion, romance novel, lingerie catalog, latex or nonlatex gloves, sex toys, nipple clamps, mirror, or your credit card if you're buying porn or access to sex-related chat communities. If your masturbation requires the Internet, make sure your connection is quick— as a friend of mine (Debby's) once said, dial-up internet connections should come with Viagra.

Consider cleanup Supplies aren't just for fun times—they're also for what comes next: the cleanup. Having tissues or a towel nearby can put your mind at ease when you're about to

If you require the Internet, make sure your connection is quick—dial-up connections should come with **Viagra**

blow or leak. Women who experience female ejaculation (i.e., who "squirt") in large amounts may feel more confident if they lay a towel on their bed—that is, if they're concerned about getting that much wetness on their sheets or in their mattress (some women love it). Some men prefer to do it on a towel, too—or to get off in the shower, for ease of clean-up.

Ready your body First, clean your hands. Second, if your fingers are going inside your vagina or butt, make sure your nails are filed down—no sharp edges. Nail files are far better for this than biting your nails or clipping them. You might also want to go to the bathroom prior to your trip down masturbation lane. Although some women and men report greater sexual stimulation when they have a full bladder, others are distracted by the need to pee. If anal self-play is in the cards, a preplay trip to the bathroom may help as well. Some men and women even give themselves a pre-anal-sex-play enema.

Find your alone-time

Get your privacy by whatever means necessary: Shut your pet out of your bedroom, switch off your cell phone (unless you're using it as part of masturbation), and lock your doors. Turn music up enough to drown out the sounds of your annoying neighbors. You don't need unwelcome visitors when you're in the throes of solitary pleasures.

Get into the zone

It's difficult to get off if you're thinking about work or the upcoming marathon you're training for—unless those things do it for you. Most of us need to get into some kind of sex zone, whether it's thinking about a current or past partner or a particularly hot scene or image from your favorite source of erotica (think: porn, swimsuit catalog, romance novel). Or you could invent your own "what if?" scenario. What if you had suggested to that good-looking passenger sitting next to you on the plane/train that you pop into the bathroom for a quickie? What if you ran into your ex at a bar and had crazy sex in the bathroom? What if you walked into your hot

coworker's office, locked the door behind you, and then went down on him or her—and then you got caught by your boss, who looked disappointed only for an instant before making you pleasure her or him in exactly the same way? In masturbation world, everyone is sexy and nothing goes wrong in terms of getting hurt, infected, or fired, so give yourself a little creative license to explore.

Be wise

If you're indulging in anal self-play, you may want to slip a lubricated condom over your finger or sex toy, or slip your hand into a glove if these fingers or toys will next go into your mouth or vagina (if you're a woman), in order to distance yourself from fecal matter. And if you're using sex toys on any body part, make sure they're your own—not "borrowed" without asking from a partner, family member, or roommate. Remember: Only waterproof vibrators should go into the shower or bathtub—check the packaging and, if you're not sure, keep it on dry land.

Look, *no hands!*

Vibrators, dildos, shower heads, washing machines, pillows, artificial vaginas, and other hand substitutes Humans are a creative bunch—the number of objects men and women have included in their me-time is astounding. Among the definitely not recommended are beer bottles, light bulbs, shampoo bottles, vegetables, dolls, and batteries. Fortunately, some objects go quite well with masturbation, thank you.

Vibrators And they're not just for women anymore. There's a huge choice out there, with many models designed for men. If you are shy about making a purchase, remember that there are many online outlets with lots of information on each product. Go explore!

Dildos These come in a variety of materials. Some are even quite "green," in that they're made with recycled materials or hardwood (pun intended, we're assuming). Like vibrators, dildos with a wide base can be pleasurably inserted into the vagina or anus.

Shower heads In the transition from childhood to adolescence, many teenagers come to look forward to their alone-time while taking a bath or shower—and not just for getting clean.

Even well into adulthood, many women and men revel in the joys of a massaging shower head or a perfectly well-placed stream of water falling from a bathtub faucet onto the breasts, penis, or vulva.

Pillows Some women and men remember having practiced kissing by kissing their pillows when they were children.

For adults, pillows may become an entirely different kind of partner—the kind you grind against or all-out hump.

For him or her In addition to vaginal and clitoral vibrators, some are made for anal play, prostate stimulation, nipple pleasure, and, of course, for tingling the penis and scrotum of many a man, thanks to vibrating cock rings.

> "There's nostalgia attached to using the shower head to get off—memories of my teenage minxish self!"

Fake vaginas When tubular in structure, these may be called masturbation sleeves and may have one hole to insert the lubed-up penis into or two holes (one at each end), so that the penis comes out the other end (the latter is good for men with long erect penises). Many different models are available online and in specialist shops. Some fake vaginas/vulvas are modeled after those of porn stars, and can be held against a wall and laid, or laid down on the bed for making sweet, sweet love to.

Clean up can involve rinsing and corn starch (which helps absorb moisture) though, which can be annoying—but perhaps worth those 30 seconds of bliss?

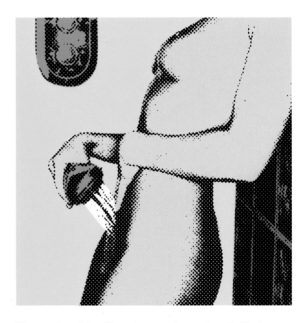

Shower-head fun If you have a shower head with a variety of settings, well, then you have an aqua vibrator of your very own. If you didn't explore the delights of the shower head in your teens, now's the time.

Chapter 4
Prepping for pleasure

Love *shack*

Pimp your bedroom When it comes to prepping your bedroom for a night of passion, it pays huge dividends to concentrate on having three core fundamentals in place: subdued or diffused lighting, clean sheets on the bed, and a generous and varied stash of condoms within easy reach. Although these points sound blindingly obvious, many sexual encounters have been marred by neglecting these basics.

Lighting for love If you wish to appear older or sinister, or to simply showcase your blemishes, stretch marks, or early onset male-pattern baldness, harsh overhead lighting is definitely the way to go. Conversely, a soft light, set at a low level, works like nature's airbrush, improving your skin tone, eliminating unflattering shadows, and maybe even spinning the clock back a few years. Make no mistake: Mitigating self-conscious thoughts will assuredly result in you and your partner enjoying sex much more. You don't have to take our word for it—a 2009 study from the University of Texas shows that women who feel better about their bodies report higher levels of sexual desire. Men feel similarly[1].

Even if you are supremely confident in your ability to look ravishing under interrogation lighting, a softer light in the bedroom is the ultimate tried-and-tested way to set the right mood for sex, and signals a little sexual savoir faire on your part. Yes, candlelight can create a great ambience and be very flattering, but will seem a little too premeditated, finicky, and precious for "opening night." Pimping out your bedroom to look like some voodoo shrine, then, is best left for long, exploratory sessions a little further down the road. To start with, keep it simple and turn on a lamp that's positioned below eye level, and that's equipped with a soft-tone light bulb.

If you wish to **appear older or sinister**, then *harsh overhead lighting is definitely the way to go*

Clean sheets, dirty mind Tousled hair, crumpled clothing, and smeared lipstick can be sexy affectations, but the bed is no place for such rock-and-roll nonchalance. Frankly, there's nothing more off-putting than vaguely fetid sheets and, if you're serious about giving and receiving a good time in bed, you'll keep tabs on when you last changed them. Make a good-faith effort to keep your sex lair ship-shape and whoever joins you in it will be concentrating on having dirty fun (rather than on the cookie crumbs exfoliating the skin on their back, or the strands of unfamiliar hair wrapping themselves around their genitals).

Beyond the cleanliness of the bed itself, it's always a good idea to air out your bedroom before the big night, and to keep it sweet smelling. Burning a scented candle in your bedroom can also be a nice touch.

Bowl of plenty Whether they're in a bowl, on a shelf, or in a nightstand drawer, always have condoms easily and readily accessible. Nothing can be more mood-killing than halting the lusty action to stomp naked around the bedroom, rifling through handbags or jeans pockets in search of an elusive little packet.

If getting your hands on a condom is an abject hassle, you're decreasing the chances of using them altogether. Be a better partner, and a better friend to yourself, by thinking ahead a little and having at least five within reach. If you're going to be hosting men in your boudoir, bonus points can be had for having a wide selection on offer—penises come in all shapes and sizes, and with varying tolerances to latex and spermicide. Women, too, can react adversely to some products, so a savvy male will at the very least offer a choice between latex and latex-free condoms. By being a prepared boy or girl scout you can avoid a stop

There's nothing more **off-putting** than *vaguely fetid sheets*, so keep tabs on when you last changed them

in play, an STI, or an unwanted pregnancy, and look like you know what you're doing, too.

Again, what you're doing here is systematically mitigating against things that can detract from an optimum sexual experience. With partners who you're more familiar with, a messy or even slightly funky bedroom won't matter nearly as much, but in the early stages, it's incumbent upon you to get him or her feeling sexy and comfortable, and ensure that you don't give or contract something nasty while you're getting nasty.

Once you've taken care of these three fundamentals, you can concern yourself with other ways in which to turn your bedroom into an adult amusement park (see If music be the food of lust, pp.78–79).

It's amazing how far a guy will go for a good time. I've been known to avoid cleaning my apartment for weeks at a time, neglecting to notice inch-thick dust, but when there's a hookup in the cards, you could eat your dinner off my bathroom floor. Not that you would.

"Hot-date prep might involve **tightening the nuts** *on my bed. It's collapsed twice during the act, which was dramatic, but a bit off-putting"*

he thinks...

I found out a little while ago

that abstaining from ejaculating for a few days before hooking up with someone made sex feel incomparably better for me. A lot of guys swear by rubbing one off just prior to a date to prevent a premature finale, but by working toward having some control over my response over time, I don't feel the need to knock one out before a date and diminish the sensation.

Before I get dressed I like to jerk off to just before the point of no return a few times while massaging my taint. When I do eventually unload later on in the evening, in company, not only does it feel amazing, but there's a lot of it and it shoots out really far! It's so impressively porno!

"I'll admit that I **depilate my ass crack***. Women seem to want to get in there so it ought to be presentable"*

"I confer with girls I'm close with about their **recent hookups** *and try to learn from other's mistakes. I'm competitive that way"*

On occasion, prior to a date with, say, the hottest woman I've recently met, I get opening night nerves, so I pop half a Viagra if things are going well. If I've misread the situation (it happens) I go to bed feeling a bit silly, pitching a tent all night.

"It's pretty simple: You need a **sexy outfit**, cute lingerie, a quick trim down there, two or three **lubricated condoms**, and a small sample-sized pack of lube"

In the hours before a date, I always go out on a run. It leaves me looking fresh, and I have a more natural pink glow in my cheeks and in my lips—kind of how I look after I orgasm. Looking like that helps me feel sexier and more confident.

If it's too early in dating to have sex, I wear big granny panties. But if there's a chance of sex, I wear sexy lingerie—not so sexy that he'll think it's all I have on my mind, but enough to get him hard when I take off my dress.

"I **masturbate** before a big date. I don't orgasm, but **arouse myself** enough to want to jump his bones, and think about it until we do it"

she thinks ...

"I stick with white wine to avoid the red lips/teeth look that screams drunk hookup rather than **appealing** date"

In one study aimed at discovering what people do before a presex date with a new partner, many women said "shower and shave," underscoring the value of a groomed appearance. Most men indicated they'd shower and check for stray hairs or clean things up down there. It's sad that, as relationships develop, people tend to become less interested in impressing their partner.

Before having a guy over, I clean my cat's litter tray and put a few cat toys away. I know some guys have a fear of dating a "cat lady" so I try to tone it down

Look yummy *in bed*

Your primping, preening, beautifying presex to-do list Some sex is spontaneous—when you jump in the shower after a run together, or when your housemate's taking a nap. Then there's the kind of sex that isn't planned in a boring way, but is anticipated, hoped for, that inspires you to ditch the last hour of work to prepare for a night of passion. There's no time to waste—you need to look, feel, and smell your best.

Take a bath or shower This should be number one on everyone's presex to-do list, especially if oral sex is on the menu. Use this time to relax, unwind, and let go of your worries. And if you want to prep yourself with the pleasures of a massaging shower head, enjoy.

Check your hair down there If you popped out to the salon for a wax or cleanup during your lunch break, all you'll need to do is check for any strays or wax globs that may have been missed earlier. Your predate grooming routine may include a range of other strategies, such as trimming, sculpting, or shaving your hair into a heart or the first letter of your partner's name—a nice touch, no?

Fine-tune your grooming Women might check if they could do with any eyebrow or upper-lip grooming. Men may want to tame facial hairs that could feel too prickly during kissing or while pleasuring their partner between her legs. Both sexes will want to check their fingernails and toenails for a manicured look and for any stray slivers that might prick when you're wrapped up together in bed.

Soften up Skin that's soft is skin that begs to be touched, then touched some more. Slather a light lotion from head to toe.

> "I love the getting ready part—choosing an outfit, putting on makeup, guessing which **sexy underwear** will drive him wild"

Dry and style your hair Wet hair can look sexy, but a mouthful of it doesn't feel that sexy. Having dry hair, styled to look gorgeous, of course, will make sex more comfortable, pose fewer distractions during foreplay or on the way to orgasm, and show you're ready to go.

Dress to be undressed There are many ways to look and feel sexy—Hefner-style robes, sparkly balconette bras, dapper suits, lace teddies, doctor or nurse costumes, bare-skinned birthday suits... choose something that you feel both comfortable and sexy in. Ladies: Step into high heels only if you can walk

confidently across the room in them. Men: Choose a fabric that breathes so you don't overheat—or oversweat.

Let yourself go (to the bathroom, that is) Women often find that needing to pee interrupts the flow of sex, so try to go beforehand. And if either of you is thinking about back-door play, you'll feel much more confident if you have a bowel movement before you set off for the evening.

Freshen your breath An absolute presex must. During sex, women are more prone to "cognitive distractions," which is science-speak for thinking about the laundry—or their partner's bad breath—in the middle of the act. Brush your teeth, tongue, and the insides of your cheeks for the tasty sex to come.

Rev yourself Just before your date, rev up with a few minutes of porn or low-level vibration to set the mood for what's to come.

Add your signature scent Use just enough cologne or perfume to add sex appeal, but not so much to seem as though you're trying too hard. Spritz the air and walk into the mist, or dab a small amount on your neck and wrists.

Lube *for the brain*

Why it's OK to indulge in that fantasy or watch that erotic movie Be grateful that we live in an era in which every type of pornography we can possibly imagine is available instantly and, often, for free. Because consuming porn no longer involves skulking around adult video or magazine stores, many more people now use it, and some glorious kinks that were previously unthinkable are now positively mainstream.

Changing sexual mores These days, all kinds of people enjoy pornography. Porn is now being consumed more than ever before, which is good news for a lot of reasons. First, the increasing number of female consumers means that the fatuous idea that men are inherently more into sex than women is being eroded. The changing demographic of porn-viewership has led to a rapidly growing supply of pornography tailor-made for female enjoyment.

Secondly, people seem to be having a better time together between the sheets. There's a chicken-and-egg relationship between the kind of sex we see in porn and the kind of sex that we engage in. Some might say it's more monkey see, monkey do, but the fact remains that the sex we're having is changing faster than ever before.

Although porn shouldn't be a yardstick by which we measure our sexual athleticism, endurance, or (ahem) body parts (see pp.40–41), it does function very well as a sex-education tool.

About 10 or 15 years ago, pornography was infinitely trickier to get hold of, and more expensive. At that time, the sex people were having was more inhibited, and less expressive and diverse, than it is today. For example, in the mid-nineties anal sex was almost regarded as a circus trick. I (Grant) knew people—or knew people who knew people—who had done it,

Porn is being consumed now **more than ever before,** which is *good news* for a lot of reasons

but suggesting it to a girlfriend would have probably gotten me a slap in the face. Nowadays, not only do I not think twice about openly suggesting anal sex to women I date, but I receive requests for it. Not everyone is a fan, but the millions of men and women who do enjoy a bit of back-door action—or any other formerly fringe sexual behavior—can thank the proliferation of porn for helping to ease their

THE IMPACT OF PORN The book *The Porn Report,* which is about the use of pornography in Australia and comprises three years of research, concludes that watching porn has improved the sex lives—and relationships— of everyday Australians. The research also found that the dangers of porn addiction, while real, affect only a tiny minority of porn users, with the majority of consumers using porn responsibly, without any negative effects on their relationships, friendships, careers, parenting responsibilities[1], and so on.

kink of choice onto the sexual menu and broaden the definition of what sex actually is. Bringing your laptop into bed with your partner to poke around on the Internet for videos and images you can enjoy together can help you enjoy your sex life that much more. Sex acts that hadn't occurred to you might strike a chord when you see them, perhaps intriguing you enough to participate in them yourself. Finally, remember that not everyone is into porn—always respect your partner's views.

Sharing fetishes and fantasies It's perfectly normal and healthy to harbor fetishes and fantasies. Many people fantasize about

The process of merely *sharing fantasies*, especially those that would be impractical, is **worthwhile** in itself

being tied up, or dominant/submissive role play, making a sex tape, having sex in a public place, or talking dirty, for example. It's also perfectly normal to share these fantasies or fetishes when you feel comfortable.

Create an environment of trust by first asking your partner what turns them on. Get them to describe a fantasy they've always wanted to act out. Even if it doesn't appeal to you, withhold judgment and think how good it must feel to openly share this highly personal information with you. Then, when it's your turn to list the scenarios you've always wanted to make happen, your partner will be primed to be just as accepting. With luck, you'll have similar items on your to-do lists, or maybe seeing how turned on he or she becomes while sharing their fantasy is all the incentive you need to help them indulge it. The process of merely sharing fantasies, especially ones that would be difficult, impractical, or illegal to pull off in real life, is worthwhile in itself.

Take two... *Action!*

Taking sexy pictures and videos can fast-track desire In the not-too-distant past, having an X-rated film roll developed over the counter was too embarrassing for all but die-hard enthusiasts. But the proliferation of digital cameras and camera phones today means that the amount of DIY smut floating around has exploded. Everyone, it seems, is doing it.

The world we live in is changing at a rapid pace. When I (Grant) started dating, girls who were cool with you snapping pictures of them naked—let alone *in flagrante*—were few and far between, probably because taking X-rated pictures back then involved the staff at the local pharmacy getting a tantalizing window into your sex life. Not so nowadays. If you're thinking of turning your boudoir into a mini porn set, below are some points to remember.

Lighting to flatter
Be prepared to see yourself in a way that you probably haven't before. The first time I (Grant) was confronted with what my sex face looks like, I was astounded that anyone would let me go near them.

> "I hide my favorite naughty picture of her in my wallet and **sneak a peak** at it about a billion times each day"

For the most flattering results, you're usually best off creating a softly lit environment and dispensing with the flash altogether. Another great way to get some sexy shots is to use the flash but cover it with a color gel—a piece of translucent, colored plastic. Red is perfect for imparting a sleazy, old-timey New Orleans bordello kind of vibe. Blue makes it look like you're doing it in an igloo.

Retro-style snapshots
In 2008, Polaroid announced that it was ceasing to manufacture instant film. The Impossible Project was born to pick up the slack, and Fujifilm increased their production, meaning that we can still take pervy pictures the way that our parents did

[shudder]. If you don't need to be quite *that* authentic, there are several smart phone apps that replicate the classic look, so we can take "pervaroids" for years to come.

Making movies
If you're shooting video, don't bother with a tripod. There's nothing creepier and more boring than watching a bum go up and down for 20 minutes from across a room. Take advantage of how small cameras have become and take turns passing the camera back and forth as you roll around. Warning: Only use the Paris Hilton–preferred night vision setting if you're prepared to look like something from *Children of the Damned*.

Speaking of Ms. Hilton, sex tapes do seem to have a habit of resurfacing at both convenient and inconvenient times. You can either accept the risk of that happening, and all of its ramifications, or else ensure that your identity is obscured completely.

Be a porn star If you're in front of the camera, now is not the time to be shy. Go ahead and indulge every porn-inspired fantasy you've ever had, and make the most of every exhibitionist gene in your DNA.

If music be *the food of lust...*

Why a sexy playlist is a seduction essential Music has the power to elicit very strong emotional responses in the human animal—an attribute well suited to the act of love—or lust. If chosen well, your sexy playlist can create a languid, sexually charged atmosphere that sets the scene for seduction, but a badly chosen playlist is tacky or—worse—a passion killer. So compile yours with care.

Music to have sex by... Here, people generally fall into three schools of thought. First, there are those who are meticulous about the tunes they bump to. These audiophiles masterfully hone sets designed to either cue or mirror the crescendos, plateaus, and diminuendos of the sex act. A second group is less precious about what they're having sex to. They just want to prevent their neighbors, housemates, or children hearing cries of passion, or shield their own ears from the more embarrassing sex noises that tend to arise from time to time. Lastly, there are those who happily go at it with or without musical accompaniment. After a while in a relationship, most of us end up in this third grouping. Are our sex lives the poorer for it?

Some of you may recall a time when music came on CDs. Unless you bothered to create and burn your own mixes, it was incumbent upon you to have sex-friendly albums on hand. The mind boggles to think of the countless hours of lovemaking logged during the somber, sultry tones of Portishead's *Dummy* and Massive Attack's *Mezzanine*. These albums were so de rigueur in the late 1990s and early 2000s that, for people of a certain age, individual tracks are inextricably linked to parts of the sexual repertoire. When you're a guest in a new partner's place, however, they get to be the DJ and you get to relax and (hopefully) enjoy their tunes. It's all part of the home-field advantage (see the sections My place? and Or yours?, pp.20–23)

The proliferation of MP3 files has meant that entirely sex-compatible albums are no longer necessary. So how do we best take advantage of the power technology has vested in us? We don't suggest specific songs and artists here, but offer a few general pointers, starting with what not to be listening to while getting it on.

MUSICAL TIMING It's easy to lose track in the heat of passion. Sometimes, you find out that what seemed like a marathon session actually lasted just a few minutes. Use your playlist to give you an idea of time elapsing, as a means of pacing yourself. Make out for two tracks, let your hands wander all over each other for another two, go down on your partner for a further three, and so on. It sounds incredibly formulaic, but by using music as a rough guide, you're ensuring against being a flash-in-the-pan and, ultimately, you'll be making your partner's orgasm that much more powerful and satisfying.

Avoid the overtly sexy A few songs and artists have become inextricable from the sex act—Marvin Gaye, Barry White, Al Green, and their respective hits. Now, while you may love vintage R&B as much as the next person, there's something incredibly unnerving about having sex to music that you yourself may have been conceived to. If that thought's not unsettling enough for you to extirpate such songs from your playlist, consider this: Anything that's trying to be overtly sexy is, by definition, not sexy.

Stick to a consistent tempo range
Going from a dirge to something speedy will invariably result in (hopefully) unintentional comedy. About 15 clicks either side of 100 bpm is a comfortable range—one that will accommodate both explorative foreplay and an escalation in passion.

Keep it flowing It's always best to have your musical accompaniment be one continuous piece of music. At the very least, set

The **mind boggles** to think of the *countless hours of lovemaking* logged during Portishead's *Dummy*

up your playlist so that the songs run into one another. Silence between tracks just feels weird, taking you out of the moment and making you conscious of the songs themselves.

    I (Grant) recently hooked up with a vinyl revivalist. While listening to her crackling, warm-sounding records during the act was tons of retro-fun, her getting up to put on the B side each time was less than ideal. Take advantage of the technology at your fingertips and have your playlists last for at least two hours. You know, just in case.

If food be *the fuel of lust*

Tips for picnicking in bed Because both are so sensuous, food and sex are often mixed. Logic might suggest that if each is so delightful, surely in tandem they are twice so—and yet, that's not always the case. Both can be tasty and decadent, but they can also be fraught with challenges when combined, leaving even the most well-intentioned mixologist confused about how to make it work.

As far as taking food into bed goes, consider these words from the wise for tasty, sexy—but manageable—sex play.

Honey This sugary substance can add sufficient sweetness to your sex play. However, it's also quite sticky, so you may want to dab only the smallest amounts of it onto your partner's body before licking it off. Honey is apparently good for the complexion and for dealing with skin irritations—so there are some other benefits involved, too.

Make sure you keep honey away from the vagina, as there is a risk of yeast infections developing. If honey is laced on the penis, make sure you do a very thorough job of licking it off before intercourse begins, lest it contributes to irritation or a yeast infection for her.

Chocolate syrup This childhood staple gets a new lease on life in the adult arena. Chocolate syrup is better on the breasts or penis and, as with honey, should be licked off the penis thoroughly prior to intercourse.

If you're worried about the mess, a good option is to take your sex play into the kitchen where you might be less concerned about it.

Why not turn his penis into a sexy sundae by putting on just a dab of ice cream followed by chocolate syrup and sprinkles? Here's a tip: Unless he's unusually well endowed in the girth department, flavors that have smaller bits in them (such as mint chocolate chip) work better than flavors with large chunks, such as cookie dough ice cream. Large chunks of brownie or cookie dough just don't stay on an erect penis long enough to eat them and quickly wind up on the floor.

Peanut butter Spread this on the nipples to make an excellent adhesive for chocolate nipple pasties. Make sure your partner doesn't have any nut allergies before going down this route or you could end up in the emergency room!

Make your own body sugar Try mixing savory herbs such as basil with powdered sugar. It's easy to make your own flavored body sugar at home. Add about a quarter to half a teaspoon of your preferred herb or other flavor and mix well with about two tablespoons of powdered sugar. It doesn't keep well, so try to use it up that same night.

Remember: no food on condoms It may not seem unwise, but it is. Condoms are not designed to withstand contact with chocolate syrup, honey, champagne, frosting, or other foods. If you're using condoms, limit your food play to foreplay and wash the penis thoroughly before intercourse. Or just use food for nongenital play.

It's intriguing how food leads people to bed. Some chefs encourage seduction by serving desserts that couples have to use their fingers to build or to eat. Assembling a dessert tower or dipping strawberries into chocolate encourages you to become comfortable with getting a little dirty, which can be very sexy, as can licking each other's fingers or dabbing whipped cream off your partner's chin.

"A final word to the wise: Even the most careful bed picnics can get messy. Keep some wipes handy"

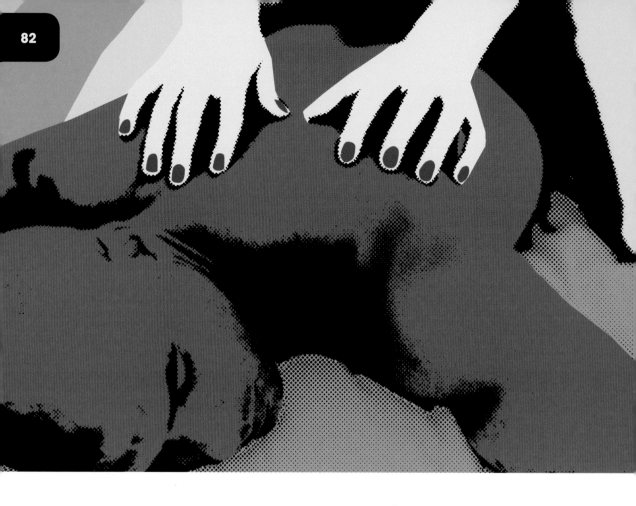

Different *strokes*

Massage techniques to prime you for pleasure Massage isn't for everyone, but when you're both really into it, it adds even more sensuality to sex. Taking the time to delight one another's bodily senses and heighten desire is an art form—and an indulgence. And it is quite a treat to have your partner lying naked, face-down, eagerly awaiting your seductive, sexual, playful touch.

Giving Although you can touch each other without any products, using lotion, massage oil, or water-based lubricant makes it slicker in a good way. Bear in mind that oils can cause latex condoms to tear. Massage mitts give extra sensation through ridges or textured nubbins. Some are even sold with companion vibrators.

When you massage down your partner's back, spend time around his or her behind. Applying firm pressure here can indirectly stimulate the genitals, particularly if you gently but firmly press their pelvic area into the mattress. You might even slip your fingers between your partner's thighs to check how erect he is or how wet she is.

Not that you're ready for sex yet—surely, you'd like at least a little more sex play, yes? On average, men and women both say they'd like about 20 minutes of foreplay before intercourse[1].

In addition to the typical back/neck/butt massage, incorporate frontal touch. Breast massage can be highly pleasurable (82 percent of women find that breast and/or nipple play causes or enhances their arousal[2]), but breasts rarely get the attention they deserve. Start with the most sensitive parts of the breasts, the tops and bottoms, working your way slowly toward the nipples. Using lotion or lubricant can change the way your touch feels. If you're trying this in the shower, lather her breasts with soap for a more slippery, lavish feel.

> "Afterward, she cleaned me up with a warm, wet towel and gave me a happy ending. It was sublime"

Receiving If you're the one being massaged, relax and let your cares slip away. Most people probably wouldn't have a problem with that idea, but if you're the type that's never been much for touching or being touched, you might be able to change your perspective on it if you think of how much your partner wants to get to know your body intimately.

Don't be afraid to make yourself comfortable—this massage is for you, after all. If your partner is being too firm or too gentle with their touch, ask for a different kind of touch, pace, or depth. Choose music that helps get you in the mood, or slip into massage after a bath, shower, or long run—whatever helps you relax and embrace touch and intimacy.

Be experimental Tease your partner with different types of touches and licks, perhaps a few nibbles along his back, neck, forearms, butt cheeks, and thighs. Maybe shimmy your breasts down his back and legs.

Massage oils Massage oils are often infused with a heady, sexy scent and can feel—and look—amazing on the skin. But they are messy, so keep a warm, wet washcloth nearby if you choose to use them.

Men are mostly gracious when women aren't feeling into sex. Whether it's because we have a headache, or we're stressed, or we're just not into it, they don't usually throw a lot of pressure our way, and when they do, we know they're in the wrong.

"Sometimes, I just want to cuddle, and other times, all I want in bed is a good book and a cup of tea"

she thinks...

When men aren't into sex,
women often don't understand. How come? It's a myth that men always want sex. Like us, they get tired, stressed, overworked, and anxious, which all have an impact on desire. Sadly, I hear from women who don't understand this. Some even accuse their partners of not loving or being attracted to them anymore, cheating on them, or of being "secretly gay."

If your partner needs a day off, let him or her know you're cool with it. Enjoy simply hanging out together on the couch, cuddling and chatting. Remember—there are reasons other than sex that keep you interested, and there's always the chance for hungry, urgent sex tomorrow.

"We spent the whole evening laughing, which was just as much fun... well, almost!"

"I was thinking if he walks in and sees me, it'll turn him on. He didn't, but just thinking about him seeing me like that did it for me"

If your man just is not in the mood and you can't or don't want to cool off, go solo—get into the bedroom and masturbate. Get reacquainted with yourself and whet your appetite for another day, when your man has his mojo back.

I've come up with some lame excuses: 'I'm allergic to cat dander' or 'I have to pick up my parents from the airport.' The truth is, I'm just not in the mood."

On the many, many occasions when a woman has declined sex with me, no explanation was necessary. I didn't cite their closet homosexuality or disseminate mild hearsay about their general oddness. I just ran off into the night.

Women have it good. They can pick and choose male sexual partners at will, and it's always resolutely acceptable for them to be uninterested in having sex at a moment's notice. This is not the case for men.

"I respected her good judgment and thought about getting some lifts in my shoes or doing some more push-ups"

he thinks...

"When I don't think I'll warrant a glowing review (and hopefully some referrals) I'd rather protect my brand and save it for another time"

On a few occasions I've been invited back to girls' places ostensibly for sex and, on arriving at their respective stoops, had second thoughts and gently declined their kind offer. Their befuddled expressions implored me to explain myself. In truth, I simply wasn't feeling it and, even though I could have gone through the motions, I wouldn't have been doing either of us any favors.

Chapter 5
Love action

Kissing with *confidence*

I just want your extra time and your... If taking your partner to previously uncharted heights of ecstasy is your goal, you've got to... slow... it... down. Sex that's quick and dirty is great, don't get us wrong, but if you really want to establish yourself as a sexual master, front-loading sessions with slow, simmering passion will put you ahead of the game. All good things, it seems, do come to those who wait.

The art of kissing Don't be fooled into thinking that kissing is somehow separate from foreplay. It's the most devastating weapon in your arsenal and should be deployed before, during, and after everything else you get up to.

You see, a disproportionate amount of the brain is devoted to interpreting signals from the mouth. A study at the University of Albany hypothesized three reasons why kissing is so crucial to good sex. First, kissing plays a vital role in mate selection—we get to "know" a prospective mate chemically by the taste of their mouth and lips. Secondly, kissing promotes bonding, partly because we know that we are putting ourselves at risk of illness by kissing somebody, but also because kissing is thought to raise levels of the hormone oxytocin (the so-called "cuddle hormone") while lowering cortisol (a stress hormone). The third—and most pertinent—hypothesis is that kissing is the human way of increasing arousal and, therefore, of increasing the chances of getting it on. The study found strong scientific support for all the hypotheses, and also that more than half of men interviewed would happily have sex without any kissing taking place beforehand, while fewer than 15 percent of women would be cool with that[1]. What's the upshot of all the smooching being logged at various laboratories? Kissing is important and, if there's a female partner involved, it's incredibly important.

Make a slow but steady approach Nothing throws a wrench in the works like banging gnashers right out of the gate. You're not pecking your grandma on the cheek, either, so don't purse your lips like a cat's butthole. Visualize saying the word "prune" to get the basic lip shape and softness but, you know, don't actually say it. That would be weird.

AVOID THE KISS OF DEATH You really ought to know this already but, from all the reports of terrible kissing that we get wind of, we reckon it warrants repeating. **Brush after every meal. Floss. See your dentist every six months. Invest in a tongue scraper.** Scientific studies have shown that tongue bacteria produce malodorous compounds and fatty acids that may account for up to 80–95 percent of bad breath[2]. It's amazing to see people avoiding predate garlic like they're Nosferatu when what they've eaten is infinitely less likely to have their date recoiling than what's been allowed to fester in their mouths. If you've got no idea if you've got stank breath, lick the back of your hand (when he or she isn't looking, of course) and smell it after 15 seconds or so. If it's bad, it's time for some gum. But remember that gum is just temporarily covering the underlying problem and it's also not ideal if you're sharing a bottle of something delicate and expensive.

Leave your tongue and saliva in your own head for the time being. Introduce it too soon and you're robbing yourself of an opportunity to intensify the passion a little later on. At first, you're just exploring. Feel his or her lips with your own. Suck their bottom lip into your mouth slightly, roll it around a little. As all this exploratory work is going on, intensify the excitement by allowing your hands to wander—brush her hair from her face, place your hands around her waist or on his shoulders, grab a handful of his hair. On paper it all sounds a bit like a love scene from a Merchant Ivory film, but you're giving yourself a nice, long runway from which to take off.

Okay, so now you can start thinking about Frenching. This is not a competition to see how far you can get your tongue down one another's

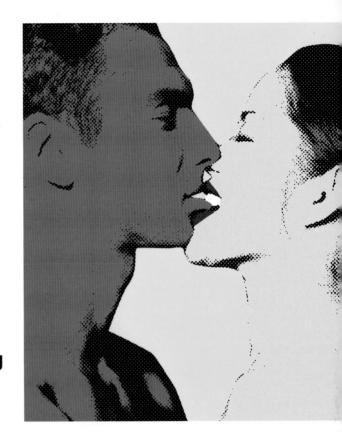

Kissing, the most **devastating weapon in your arsenal,** should be deployed _before, during, and after everything_

throats—that's best left for when you're having dirty sex a little later on. For the time being, you're just going to carry on with the kissing, only you've opened your mouth and are giving a little bit of tongue. From there you can take turns visiting each other's mouths. Avoid all jabbing, stabbing, or circular motions (as if your mouth is set on a spin cycle). The idea is to tease, tantalize, titillate. Be sure to come up for air every now and then. An effective palate cleanser is to get your mouth into the side of his or her neck. If you're over the age of 25, however, hesitate before giving or receiving a hickey. A nibble, nuzzle, or lick is more than sufficient. Combine this escalation in the action by drawing the other person closer and, if you've played your kissing cards right, the next event will be that much more explosive.

Breast *behavior*

Is more than a mouthful a waste?

No breast is ever a waste. Small ones fit easily into a partner's mouth; large ones spill beautifully over cupped hands or corsets. Research suggests that larger breasts tend to be less sensitive, while those of smaller cup sizes (A and B) tend to be more sensitive. And on the subject of sensitivity, the most responsive part appears to be the tops of the breasts—not the nipple.

Women's breasts come in an enormous range of shapes and sizes. Their perkiness (like the perkiness of men's penises) changes over time—a natural occurrence, and one that doesn't make breast play any less sensual. Make sure she knows how beautiful her breasts are and how lucky you are to be touching, kissing, groping, or sliding your penis in between them, and sex will be (much) better for it.

Grab a handful Masters and Johnson noted that women's breasts grew larger when they were feeling sexually excited or aroused. And Kinsey found that, of the thousands of women his research team interviewed, 11 percent frequently stimulated their breasts as part of masturbation[1]. Basically, by giving the breasts their due attention, you're onto a winner.

Women report that sensation is richest along the tops, bottoms, and sides of the breasts. This is a very good thing, as it provides more surface area for breast play, something that most women find enhances their sexual arousal[2].

And play you should! We recommend massaging her breasts—grabbing them gently and circling the sides, or encircling her from behind in the shower and offering her a more slippery, erotic breast massage. Often, the nipple is focused on to the neglect of the rest of the breast. Try massaging the breast in its entirety. Trace your fingers gently around your partner's breasts. If you're a woman, do this to yourself, or ask your partner to use his or her tongue to glide around your breast in search of the most sensitive and erotic spots. A firm massage will produce one sensation; a feather-light touch or warm air blown gently on or around the nipple will result in another. See what feels good to you or your partner.

Breast seduction There are numerous additional ways to include your breasts in sex play. Why not:
- Dress your breasts up in a seductively cut balconette bra or a striking push-up bra or lingerie set
- Text or email your partner with a picture of your breasts as a hint of what's to come later
- Add to your breasts' allure by lacing them with shimmery cream that catches the light—and consequently catches the eye
- Make your breats even fancier with bejeweled or tasseled nipple pasties or jewelry (no piercings required—some jewelry products hang simply over the nipple)
- Lay on top of your partner and drag your breasts over their face, chest, and all the way down to their thighs.

"Some people report that **nipple piercings** heighten sensitivity, while others say they decrease it"

"Few women experience orgasm through breast stimulation alone, but it may be worth a try—if only for the fun and novelty. There's nothing wrong—and plenty right—with spending an entire sex session playing with her breasts. Give them your undivided attention—and let her know how much you enjoy doing it. She may experience orgasm or something close to it and, if not, let her beg for whatever takes her to the next level, be that oral sex, intercourse, or a spanking."

Nipple *tips*

Nipple play Nipples are one of the body's erogenous zones, and should never go unattended by any partner worth their salt. Although women's nipples tend to be more sensitive, men, too, can find nipple play arousing. Not everyone enjoys the same level of nipple stimulation, though, so it's a good idea to start with a gentle lick or caress and gauge your partner's reaction before taking it to the next level.

Tweaking the dial

If your partner finds that nipple stimulation enhances their arousal, try touching or even lightly pinching his or her nipples as orgasm approaches. For some people, this is just enough to send them over the orgasmic edge.

And for reasons we cannot explain, it seems that some people who enjoy nipple stimulation also seem to be into stimulation of their ear lobes. Ask (or try) to find out if that's true for your partner. You could be missing a trick.

Also, consider flavored nipple creams, which are available through many sex boutiques and home sex-toy parties. These can make for better (and tastier) breast play.

Nipple clamps

These are one of the lesser-known sex toys on the market. Some people opt for state-of-the-art vibrating nipple clamps. Others make use of clothespins borrowed from their laundry room. If you or your partner dig nipple play, a handy nipple clamp can provide constant stimulation while your hands explore elsewhere.

Nipple play for him

In one study, about half of men reported that nipple stimulation causes or enhances their arousal. However, some guys have never even tried rubbing or pinching their nipples, perhaps thinking of it as a more "feminine" part of sex. To make the most of each other's bodies, try licking his nipple as you travel over his body with kisses. Another option is to reach up and rub or gently pinch his nipples while you're going down on him. Or try a gentle bite—it might provide him with a thrill.

The spice of life

Nipples and areolas (much like vulvas and penises) come in an array of colors and sizes. They can be small and dark, small and pale, large and dark, large and pale, or somewhere in between. Spend time on a topless beach sometime and bask in the diversity, knowing that they all taste and feel equally delicious.

And one more for good measure...

Perhaps you've heard of people having "third nipples." One study found that about six percent of patients in a given clinic had a third nipple (called a "supernumerary nipple") so don't be surprised if you come across one. Embrace it as you would any other interesting quirk or characteristic of your partner. Given that they tend to be smaller and less well developed, they're typically not all that sensitive during sex play. However, if your partner asks for a lick or a tug, we hope you'll be open to it.

Nipples
are
highly
sensitive to
touch—according
to one study, 59
percent of women have
asked their partners to
stimulate their nipples
during sex. During sexual
arousal, muscles throughout the
body contract via a process called
myotonia. The contraction of
internal smooth muscle in the
nipple is what causes
women's nipples to
become erect during
arousal or when cold. A
fun fact: Myotonia is also
responsible for the uterus
lifting during arousal (making
room in the vagina), toes
curling during orgasm—
and the facial
contortions known
as "the O Face."

"I slide my teeth gently around my partner's nipple and lightly flick it with my tongue. It drives him wild"

Hand-job *heaven*

Dispensing pleasure hand over fist If you think giving a hand job is just a case of gripping his penis and pumping your fist for a minute or two, you're right. Giving a knee-trembling hand job that he'll fondly recall in the autumn of his years, however, is as nuanced, sensual, and ornate as your imagination permits. Techniques can be mastered, and he really won't mind you practicing on him—so get cracking.

What are you working with? Don't go grabbing around for his penis too soon. Make out, grope each other through clothing, dry hump, and say a few nasty things to make sure he's feeling incredibly constricted down there. When he's got a thumping hard erection, unbutton his jeans or pants and pull them down his hips.

It should take only a quick glance to figure out if your man friend is circumcised or not. Playing with a circumcised penis requires a slightly different technique than an unmodified specimen. When left as nature intended, a lot of the pleasure from a hand job derives from the foreskin sliding over the sensitive head or glans. On a modified member there is nothing between glans and administering hand, so snipped guys will appreciate something to ease the motion. Lube is ideal but saliva is a great all-natural alternative. Once it's out and standing at attention for you, it's a nice touch to pay it a compliment. A simple "Wow," "Nice," or an anticipatory "Mmmm" will do the trick.

Get ambidextrous Find a position in which you can continue kissing and get all ten fingers involved in pleasuring his unit. If you're right handed, use your left hand to cradle and/or gently jostle his balls and the right to give a few standard strokes with a grip of medium firmness. Once you've got his attention, switch your grip from regular (how you'd hold a banana) to

Find a position in which you continue kissing, but can get **all ten fingers involved** in **pleasuring his unit**

overhand (how you'd shoot dice). Now, as you go from the base to the head, smoothly bend at the wrist so that you're working his whole penis in a spiral motion. Once you've got the motion of going up, down, and around, experiment with applying more pressure at the base or at the top. And with your slippery left hand, try making a circle of your thumb and index finger above his balls and gently but firmly pull downward.

Now that you've shown him you know your way around the neighborhood, it's time to give him the ol' razzle dazzle.

Squid With your nondominant hand firmly grip the base of his penis and pull it downward and slightly away from his body until it feels like it wants to spring back upward. Place the tops of all four fingers and the thumb of your dominant hand on the tip of his glans and run them up and down the top of his penis, until the head comes into contact with your palm. Your fingers should make a motion like a squid's tentacles as it propels itself through water.

Twist-off With your nondominant hand make the Vulcan hand gesture (a V shape by spreading the middle and ring fingers) and put the base of his penis snugly in the notch. With your other hand, make the motion of twisting the screw cap off of a bottle. Begin with a gentle motion, preferably with a bit of lube.

Ring This is the same as a standard hand job but, instead of creating a cylinder of all four fingers and thumb, just make a circle of your thumb and index finger. This is particularly good-feeling on the ridge of the glans or corona.

Tug of war Straddle his lap and get plenty of lube on his piece. Then, with a hand-over-hand motion, pull your hand from the base of

Envelop his penis in the space _between your palms_ and experiment with **how much pressure** you apply

his penis to the tip. As one hand releases at the tip, the other starts at the base. You can pretend you're pulling something toward you on a rope if you like.

Volley-ball grip Interlace your fingers as if about to pop a ball over the net. Envelop his penis in the space between your palms and experiment with the amount of pressure applied.

Hand-bang Lay on your back and press your slippery hands together in front of your heart. He'll put his knees on either side of your rib cage and push his penis between the heels of your hands. All you have to worry about is the pressure of your opposing palms as he does all the work. You just MacGyvered him an auxiliary vagina! How clever.

Slips of *the tongue*

The art of the blow job With age and experience, fewer men are content just to have someone put their mouth on their penis. If all they wanted was a warm mouth, they might pay a sex worker, entice a pet dog with strategically placed peanut butter, or screw themselves silly with a lubed-up pocket pussy shaped like a mouth. (We're not recommending these but, suffice to say, it's a wild world out there.)

Enthusiasm matters What men want is a blow job from someone who wants to give them a blow job, who will take his penis in their mouth and look up with a smile on their lips—not from someone emulating a bored porn star. If you're not into it, and can't get into it no matter what, don't do it. Frowning and gagging your way through something that should be a pleasurable, exciting, hotter-than-watching-premium-subscription-porn experience is a downer.

If you're into it, though, you've won half the battle. Ask to go down on him. Tell him you need a taste. Touch and arouse his penis for several minutes before slipping it into your mouth, lest the beginnings of your blow job seem more like mouth-to-mouth resuscitation than a steamy sex act. Giving a blow job can be incredibly hot—not just for him, but for you. Having a hard penis in your mouth can be highly sexy and just the thing to make you feel wet and throbbing for penetration. A blow job can be not only sexy, but educational. It's a front-row seat to seeing and feeling with your mouth how individual moves, licks, breaths, or warm air have the potential to make him so hard that he bursts at the seams.

So back to him. Once he's hard and ready for the blow job, try to muster sufficient saliva to make it wet. There's no shame in getting some spit right on his shaft to make it wetter and more slippery. It'll make sliding your mouth up and down it slicker and, likely, more arousing (and

Men want a blow job from someone who *wants to give them a blow job,* who will **look up with a smile** on their lips

more arousing translates into a firmer erection and easier orgasm for him). Use the following tips as you develop your technique.

Twisted mister Suck up and down his shaft while twisting one or both hands (depending on his length) along the base of his penis.

THE CUM FACTOR It's a big question—will he be coming in your mouth? Talk to him first and figure it out. If he will, will you **spit** it out into a towel **or swallow** it down? Another option is to have him let you know when he's about to come (many men do this out of courtesy, no matter what). That gives you the chance to decide if you're going to duck out of the way and let him come in your or his hand, on a towel, your breasts, or some other place. There's no shame in avoiding his explosion—many guys come into a towel during their own masturbation, recognizing that the sticky factor can cause a tricky clean-up. What matters more is that you find a way to please him that also pleases you.

Circle of love Circle one or both hands along the base of his penis, gripping it hard. Use your tongue to circle around the nerve-rich head of his penis. Your lips stay closed around the head.

Slow and steady In the heat of the moment, it's all too easy to go for the fast and furious approach to blow jobs. And yet many men crave long, slow licks and/or sucking, which gives them greater opportunity to focus

Having a **hard penis** in one's mouth can be just the thing to make you feel *wet and throbbing for penetration*

on their arousal and sustain their erection. The slower pace also gives your jaw a break, which can help you to suck for longer.

The whole shebang Start by kissing up his shaft, offering the occasional lick along it, or a tongue flick along his frenulum. Once you get into your preferred sucking position, make sure to give attention to his testicles—either by using your fingers to touch or roll them around or by taking mouth breaks to suck them. Another option is to continue sucking while pressing your knuckle or fingers in between his scrotum and anus, thus indirectly stimulating his prostate.

Moving on Keep in mind that many men find it difficult to ejaculate from receiving oral sex. After all, the mouth doesn't feel much like the other parts of the body they're used to (hands/vagina) and their bodies can take time to figure out how to explode in response to sucking and kissing. Be patient. If it doesn't seem like he's going to come from oral, move on to something else that's more of a slam dunk sex move.

Finger *linger*

Show her your handiwork Whether it's a furtive rub on a packed dance floor, a transgressive session under a blanket on a plane (hopefully not amid the shocked, vociferous complaints of the prude sitting behind you), or a long, steamy session in the controlled environment of your bed, digital manipulation is a much appreciated item in the program. Give it its due... and profit!

Delay gratification Instead of squishing your hand into her skinny jeans, begin your handiwork outside the clothes. As you kiss her deeply, place a hand on her thigh and, after a little while, give that leg a rub and ever-so-slowly move closer to her crotch. You both know what comes next but, by drawing out the anticipation, you'll maximize the payoff. Before getting your hands on her, press your wrist or knee between her legs. She'll likely start rubbing herself against it. This is a good sign. Firmly and rhythmically rub her through the fabric of her jeans or underwear before clearing the area of constrictive clothing. You're going to need some room to work!

Think outside the box Hot, wet, snug, and inviting—of course you're going to want to put things in there. But before you do, concentrate on all the fun things to play with in the reception area. Make a scoop shape with your hand and cover the vulva with it, like you're feeding a pony a sugar lump. Then apply a little more pressure using a tiny back-and-forth or circular motion. Women have a nerve ending–rich perineum, too. Don't be shy about giving it a little circular rub. Put her natural wetness to good use and slide your fingers in, around, and between her labia, giving them a gentle pinch and a tug if you and she are so inclined. You can also separate her labia with your index and ring fingers, using your middle finger to work the star of the show.

Giving a *super-sensitive clitoris* a **direct hit** could result in you getting a reflexive kick to the throat

The pink pearl Getting this right is going to take a little bit of communication so keep your eyes and ears open. Some women's clitorises are super sensitive and giving one of those a direct hit could result in you getting a reflexive kick to the throat. Start things off by rubbing around the clit in a circle that's about as large as a quarter. Very gradually make that circle smaller and smaller. If she begins to squirm in discomfort, widen that circle a little bit and use

GRANT'S SEXPLOITS While I was busy repelling girls in my teen years, it seemed that my peers constantly had their grubby paws in each others' pants. How did I know? Friday mornings—post Thursday night "youth club"—were abuzz with innumerable reports of such acts taking place behind the gym or the theater. I was green with envy at the time, but the positive outcome of being a late bloomer is that I've yet to be desensitized to the excitement of getting my mitts on ladies' bits and I doubt that I ever will be.

that as your baseline. If she's super sensitive, you can rub the clitoral hood, which will act as a buffer between your finger and the sensitive head. If her body language seems to be imploring you to bring it on, you can get a little more tactile with the "man in the boat." Try rolling it between your thumb and finger or, imagining that her clit is a miniature version of a man's glans, give her a Lilliputian hand job.

Get stuck in You've taken the time to do a bit of prep work, so now she should be ready, able, and more than willing to host a digit or two. Start with one finger—the middle finger has ergonomic benefits a little later on. Go in and out, slowly, methodically. Get an idea of her individual geography—there's a lot of variability in there—and see what she reacts to. Many women love having their G-spot rubbed in a

Many women love having their *G-spot rubbed,* but be creative and see what evokes **the best reaction**

come-hither motion, although you are encouraged to get creative and find out what evokes the best reaction. The G-spot can be stimulated through the front wall of the vagina, about one to three inches up. For some women the G-spot is not such a big deal. Others find that they don't like it messed with at all. So explore and see which area gets a positive response. Once you've found a spot that's doing the trick and have given it some attention, think about introducing a second finger. Make it the ring finger. Not only will this make it more comfortable for you both, but it will also mean that you can rub on, around, or near the clitoris with your thumb, which should remain on the outside. You can add more fingers if you think it will go over well, but stuff it too tight with digits and you may find you're stealing your penis's thunder.

The end If you intuit that she's approaching orgasm, continue what you're doing unless told otherwise. Some women become super sensitive in the immediate aftermath, while others are ready for a second, third, or fourth go. Read the signs and use your best judgment regarding what to do. We trust you.

Mouth *to south*

Oral techniques to give her a rush Your unbridled enthusiasm for performing oral sex on her will not go unappreciated. However, as much as you want to shove your greedy face between those silky smooth thighs, the best thing you can do to maximize her enjoyment of your oral attention is to do your prep work. Get her riled up to the point of shoving your head down there with all her might, then you're ready to begin.

Address the area When you're confident that she's good and slippery, make a measured approach to giney town. Really spend some time kissing her thighs and mons. If you have the restraint, leave her underwear on for a minute or five; kiss her parts through them, pull them slightly to one side and run your tongue along the area where the very top of her inner thigh meets her groin. Grab the fabric of her panties between your lips and pull your head back. Then release your hold and let her dampening underwear ping back onto her swelling labia. You know it's time to get to it when her horniness is beginning to be eclipsed by her frustration.

Making contact Get in a position where you have full access to her clitoris, vaginal opening, perineum, and anus. This might mean slipping a cushion under her hips and/or applying some weight to her thighs with your hands to tilt her pelvis forward. Going down on her with her panties pulled to one side is pretty punk rock, but soon it's going to become a hindrance. Whip them off of her and take a second to admire the view. Then, with a flat tongue, lick upward from her perineum to her mons, slower than you had thought possible. We're talking about taking a full 15 seconds to cover the distance. Break contact. Reset and do it again, just as slow. After about 8 to 10 of these, turn your head sideways and make out with her pussy. Like a

You know it's time to **get to it** when her *horniness is beginning to be eclipsed by her frustration*

kiss at a school dance, make it good and sloppy; explorative. Really roll her labia around here. Pretend you're Mick Jagger making out with Angelina Jolie during a morphine binge. That's the feel you're going for.

Know what you're working with Some clitorises are incredibly sensitive. Others can take quite a tongue lashing. Your first long licks should have given you a feel for what you're working with. If it's a sensitive one, work your flat tongue around it. Lick over the hood that covers the head of the clitoris. The more sensitive the clitoris, the less pressure you want to apply to it. If you're up against one that can take a thrashing, you'll get better results from making your tongue pointier and adding more pressure. Roll your tongue over and around the clit. There's no need to flutter it like a cobra. Instead keep the motion constant and regular.

Call for back up At some point, you can see if she likes having your fingers join in. Start by inserting your middle finger, palm facing up, into her vaginal opening. Graze the opening's perimeter. This area is rich in nerve endings. While continuing to lick on and/or around the head of her clitoris, gently slide that solitary finger in farther, brushing the front wall of her vagina. You'll feel a textured patch—this is the G-spot. Rub this area in a come-hither motion. You may detect a change in breathing or the noises she makes. Stay conscious of this; it's how you'll get her to where she wants to go. After some time, you can introduce the ring finger, which will likely elicit a positive response. With your tongue working the clit and the fingers of one hand rubbing her G-spot, you can place your free hand on her mons and apply a little pressure. You'll be effectively applying pressure to the same area from inside and out, here. Use a finger on the outside hand to pull back the clitoral hood slightly and expose more of the clitoral head. If you want

You may detect a *change in breathing or her noises.* Stay with this; it's how you'll get her **where she wants to go**

to get really crafty, ease the pinky of your G-spot-rubbing hand into her bum. You are now covering all the bases and would be forgiven for feeling a little proud of yourself. But it's not over 'til it's over.

In conclusion How long you spend on oral depends on the woman in question, how turned on she is, how much preparation you put in, and a whole host of other variables. Just keep at it. You'll have an idea about when her orgasm is approaching because things will usually get very quiet for about 20 seconds, you'll feel her vagina tighten around your fingers, and then she'll get a lot more vocal about how it's all feeling for her. Unless she gives a directive such as "faster," "harder," "deeper," etc., keep what you're doing fairly constant, even if she's thrashing about on the bed like a woman possessed.

For some women the whole vulva area may become too sensitive to touch postorgasm. Others will be able to have more. Until you know what she likes, keep going until she either pulls your head away or tells you to stop. There: Wasn't that fun?

Blowing each other *away*

Go into orbit on a 69 A bit of poking around on the Internet reveals that the 69 position—in which you and your partner give and receive oral sex at the same time—is quite a polarizing topic. The main complaint seems to be that it's difficult to concentrate on both the task at hand and your own pleasure when you are simultaneously the administrator and the recipient of oral affection. We say poppycock!

If you can walk and chew gum at the same time, fully enjoying a 69—or *soixante-neuf* if you're French, pretentious, or both—is well within your grasp. A great way to mitigate against cognitive dissonance is to stop thinking about the goal of orgasming and/or bringing your partner to orgasm and concentrate instead on the sensuousness—and inherent raunchiness—of the time-honored position in its many forms.

This way up In the 69's most popular and heterosexual incarnation, the gentleman is lying down. The woman is straddling the man's chest, facing his feet, and lining up her vulva with her man's mouth. Unless there's a remarkable difference in their respective heights—if he's a jockey and she's a basketball player, say—this should put her in the perfect position to pop

her partner's penis in her mouth. (If height disparity is an issue, she can experiment with how far up the man's torso she plants her knees.) Most men would agree that this setup affords him both an amazing view as well as unfettered access to his partner's vagina and anus: A pillow or cushion behind his head and neck will make his dining experience that much more comfortable. The man's hands and fingers are free to explore the vulva and anus of the woman or splay her cheeks farther to give him even better access and her the exhilarating feeling of being utterly exposed. The ladies don't have to feel like they're constantly bobbing for apples in this configuration: If it gets uncomfortable or you need a break, get your lips and tongue on his balls and use one hand to stroke his saliva-slick penis while you support your weight with the other.

About face If you're a doubting Thomas and have only tried 69ing this way in the past, you might very well find that trying it the other way around—man on top—will make an ardent believer of you. Not only will this topsy-turvy version mean that the man's mouth lines up more neatly with the clitoris; it may also result in the woman fitting a lot more of his penis in her mouth. Perfect if he relishes "deep throat" action or if she gets a special thrill at the thought of being able to take a penis to the hilt. Furthermore, the woman will now be perfectly placed to explore his balls, perineum, and anus with her fingers and mouth.

Sidewinder From here, there are several more fun ways to shut each other up. They all depend on the amount of energy, strength, and ingenuity you can muster. A lazier, but no less enjoyable version of the 69, can be had by each partner lying on their side. Access can be optimized by bending the leg nearest the ceiling and planting your foot behind the knee of your straightened leg. It all sounds a bit like a game of Twister, but once you're hankering for your partner to get fully stuck in, you'll intuitively know what to do.

> "There is a *beautiful symmetry* to going down on someone while they are *going down* on you"

Straight up If you've been doing your squats you could try your hand at a standing 69. A good way to get into it is for the woman or smaller/weaker partner to lie on a bed or table, with her head slightly off of it. The gent merely has to pop his peter in her mouth; the woman brings her legs up to his shoulders and he can grab her hips and pull her hips up to his mouth like he's about to feast on a big ol' cantaloupe. If you're the stander, it's important to keep a slight bend in the knee and, if you're feeling a bit wobbly or maybe even a little too tipsy, it's a good idea to put your partner down and opt for something less physically demanding. You could try versions of the upright 69 in both sitting and kneeling positions for instance.

With giving oral sex being as much of a turn on as receiving it, a 69 is a positive feedback loop that doesn't need a definitive conclusion to be on the sexual menu. What's more, it's easy to do and a pleasure for both parties. Chow down!

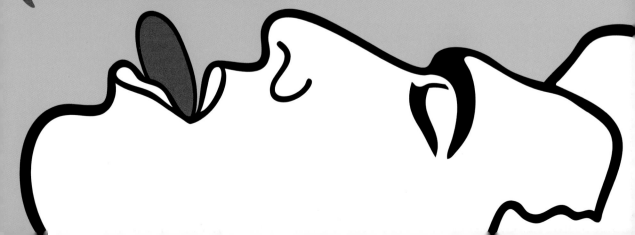

Asking *nicely*

Polite ways to request that sexual favor This probably doesn't come as a big surprise, but people don't particularly enjoy being "asked" for sex, as in the boring old "can we have sex?", which sounds completely devoid of, well, anything sexy at all. So what's a horny man or woman to do? How to make one's desires known without turning one's partner off from the possibility?

As long as you can read your partner's cues and get a sense of whether they're remotely interested in sex, asking wordlessly can be memorably sexy. If you're watching a movie, why not lay your feet in their lap and brush against their penis or vulva, hinting at what you'd like to do? For couples who are tied to their laptops while in the same house, try sending a chat message, email, or text that simply says "Feel like sex?" There are endless ways to ask for sex that are unlikely to offend and very likely to turn on.

You don't even have to ask specifically for anything; saying what you'd like to do can get your point across in a pinch. Try "I wish we were naked together" or "Want to go and play upstairs?" Or, in response to your partner asking

> "I find that 'I'd love to lick your penis' and 'feel like more orgasms today?' always elicit a good response"

what you'd like for dinner, answer "You. Now." Cheesy? Entirely. Effective? More than you'd expect. Even if your partner isn't thinking about sex, your suggestion might get their mind going—and you may soon be naked in bed together.

Now, if you're asking for a sex act you've never tried together, it can be difficult—but it's sometimes better to bring it up than spring it on your partner midaction. Blame it on a book or TV show. Tell them what you've heard and are curious about. Worried about the reaction? Start by saying "This is difficult for me to bring up, but..." which often elicits a compassionate response. If they're not into it, move on. If there's an opening, well... those who ask often receive.

Join your partner in the shower Surprise him or her with your unexpected presence. Squat down and begin licking their parts to see where it takes you. Things may get steamier than usual in there.

Get naked Try getting up off the sofa and walking to the bedroom, tossing off items of clothing provocatively along the way. Or perhaps treat your partner to an impromptu striptease for a memorable quiet night in.

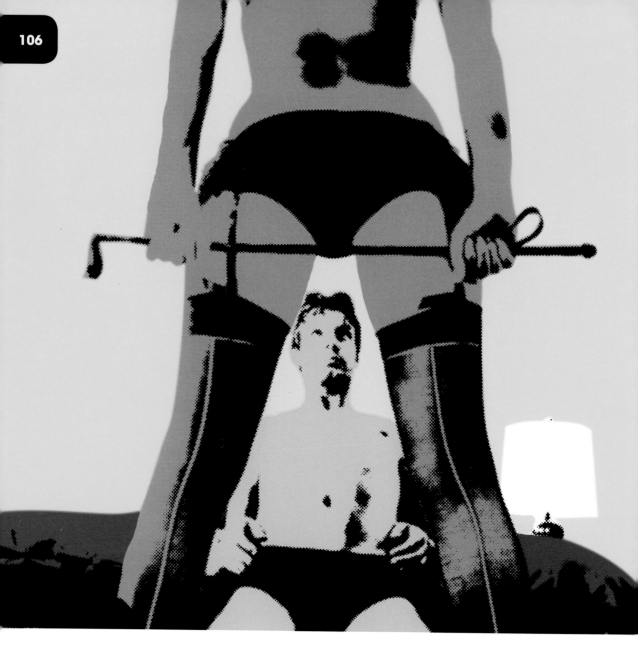

Asking *nastily*

Dirty talk to inspire depravity Sometimes, nay, oftentimes, sex is best at its most animalistic. When you're throwing one another around the room, leaving bite and scratch marks, tearing off clothing, it simply wouldn't be right to accompany your barely containable lust with sweet nothings or polite requests. But when it comes to dirty talk, it's best to start off mild and work your way up in increments of raunchiness.

When it's time to turn the air blue by saying exactly what's on your reptilian mind, you don't want the police alerted, so you do have to intuit the level of filth your partner is comfortable hearing and exceed it only slightly.

> *"The things he said got me* **so excited.** *I had no idea being submissive could be* **such a turn on"**

Blue labels The post office; the supermarket; dinner with your partner's parents—probably not the time or place to be too liberal with the c-words, or any other dirty words. Dirty sex, however, is absolutely the appropriate time to let her rip. If you have a favorite word or phrase you find exciting when referring to your respective body parts, say it like you mean it. Nervously mumbling "Your... um.... is so...um... big/wet/hard/tight" will seriously undermine any nasty vibe you're trying to create. Say it with vigor and conviction. Filthy talk, when mumbled, sounds creepy. Always. Also, you get no points for

I'm the boss! Don't be shy about saying what you want, provided it's legal, of course. Even if your partner's not that into it, an experienced bedmate will know that entertaining your whims will pay dividends soon enough.

originality in this setting, so avoid any references to "love caves," "meat truncheons," "vertical smiles," etc. They just sound silly.

Who's the boss? If you've yet to establish who is the more dominant or submissive, a round of knock down, drag out, downright rude humping is a golden opportunity. Start calling the shots and take note of how eagerly he or she obliges you. Ease into the role of tyrant by wrapping your diabolical demands in compliments: "put that beautiful ass in the air" or "stroke that gorgeous cock for me." You'll figure out how happy they are to serve by the speed and vigor with which they obey your orders. From there, mention your requests, starting with your mildest and moving up: "Lick my balls" or "suck that clit" are great opening gambits.

GRANT'S SEXPLOITS If you're not worried about what you call things but feel your partner might be, brusquely grab a body part and ask them what they call it. I once dated a girl for whom the word "pussy" was "too porno." I didn't mind either way but, by employing the aforementioned technique, we quickly settled on calling it her "coochie." (She, incidentally, referred to my penis as a "prick," which I couldn't abide. To me, "prick" sounds like a little needle—precisely the sort of association I want to avoid.)

Men can't read minds so we love it when women aren't shy about asserting themselves in bed. It shows that they know what they like and it saves a lot of messing around trying to do something that they're not into. A bit of guidance helps everyone.

"I logged **jaw-numbing** hours of cunnilingus on a girl I dated **before she told me** that she didn't like the way I did it"

he thinks...

Get to know him Pop culture representations would have you believe that men are all pretty much the same in their sexual desires and responses. Not true! Don't stereotype your man. Give him the latitude to be himself in the sack and you'll reap the rewards. Asking him what he likes is the fastest, most effective way to press his buttons and have him thinking about sex he had with you for years to come.

If you really want to turn a guy off, agree to sex when you're not really into it. When we think that you're just going through the motions, we wonder whether it's worth the effort. On the flipside, letting us know how much you're enjoying yourself is pretty much a guaranteed turn-on.

"There is nothing sexier than a woman who **initiates sex**. Enthusiasm is key!"

"Being game for almost anything and upping the ante is hot. A woman **ramping up the raunchiness** is the ultimate turn-on for me"

Don't ever think that you shouldn't share a fantasy or a whim. Chances are that we are up for it, too, and at worst, will be flattered you asked. My most memorable sexual experiences have been ones that were unexpected, raunchy, and/or risky.

"He was so gentle, yet so filthy! *I'm still not sure how he managed it... but I do know that he is definitely* the most memorable notch on my bedpost*"*

The skin covering men's genitals, coupled with the mind-boggling hydraulics of the penis that result in firm erections, mean that guys can not only take, but actually often like, firm pressure and a fast pace. Treating women's genitals the same way can spell disaster.

Women have sensitive vulvas that often require greater care—at least to start with. The clitoris is rich with nerve endings. Slamming into it with a feverish, fumbling finger can be a huge turn-off.

"I felt more pummeled than teased, *but I told him how I like it and, surprisingly, he was glad I offered up the info"*

she thinks ...

"I like a bit of rough treatment *down there sometimes, but I need to* build up to it *very slowly"*

There is a place for rough play, but until you know her likes and dislikes, keep to sensuous touch, lest she wonder if you're trying to hurt her rather than arouse her.

Venus vs. Mars It's often said that we treat our partner's bodies the way we like our own to be stimulated, so many men approach their partner's genitals with gusto, while many women take a slow, gentle approach to hand and oral play. This can work well for same-sex partners, but when men and women get together, it can be a case of Mars vs. Venus. Wave the white flag and communicate about preferences.

Chapter 6
Making ends meet

Pronto or take it slow?

The pros and cons of slow and fast love We humans like our movies to last for about 100 minutes, and our paperbacks to wrap up in around 300 pages. Sex, we're pleased to say, is a much more elastic activity. But which way to go—fast or slow? Let the mood o the moment itself always be your guide, but the relative merits of "lightning bolt" and "languorous" are definitely worth a discussion.

Sometimes, sex is best when it's unhurried, selfless, loving, experimental, and takes up the better part of a weekend. Other occasions cry out for frantic, animalistic sex that can be squeezed in during a commercial break or taken care of in the bathroom of a 747. Either way can be very, very good.

The slow train While it's good to know that sex doesn't have to go on all night to satisfy her, it's important to understand that the more you "front-load" your sessions with kissing, fingering, and enthused but methodical oral sex (see the previous chapter), the more primed your partner will be to get off when you finally do have intercourse. It really is a case of slow and steady wins the race.

If you have the fortitude and the wherewithal, you might want to tease him or her by denying them "it" several times and returning to kissing or giving oral sex. By doing this, you can take them to an elevated state of arousal. You finally get to drop the hammer when their screamed demands are in danger of alarming the neighbors. This is called delayed gratification and it can be a devastatingly good weapon in your sexual arsenal.

It's also worth mentioning that, with hormones coursing around your body and a naked vision on the bed, your perception of time might be a bit off. A good trick to

> You might want to tease them by *denying them "it"*; **delayed gratification** can be a devastating weapon

demarcate a mutually satisfying romp is to have your various activities roughly correspond to songs in a seductive playlist—see the box on page 78 for guidance.

HE SAYS Guys, if you're prone to popping off a little earlier than you'd like—something that affects up to 40 percent of men at one point or another—you can elongate sex sessions by playing with the sexual script, something I call the "change up." It's easy to forget that sex doesn't have to follow the linear progression of kissing, feeling up, oral, followed by a handful of your favorite positions, before the climactic finale. Like a Tarantino movie, start off in the middle and work backward and forward in the sexual narrative. Increase intensity and bring out your most trusted maneuvers when you experience a lull or plateau in proceedings, and cool things off again whenever you feel that the "point of no return" is imminent. This will not only help you stay in the game longer; it will also make you a dynamic and exciting partner.

The express Quickies are great and shouldn't be eschewed in favor of long lovemaking sessions. They can be raw, dirty, animalistic and may better express how you feel about your partner at that particular moment. (See Have-we-got-time-for-this? positions, pp.124–125.) When the mood strikes, you should absolutely take the opportunity to have some fast and furious fun. Not only will it be a naughty release; it conveys the idea to your partner that they still bring out the animal in you.

It's also worth remembering that while it's important to know how to satisfy your partner sexually, good sex doesn't always have to end in orgasm for both or indeed either partner.

While it's good not to be a *"two-pump chump,"* a **quick and dirty romp** can be just the thing

A quick bang without a climax might be a teaser for what you have in store for one another on a later occasion.

In my sexless teen years, I (Grant) picked up on the idea that men who were "bad" in bed were men who came quickly. Although I was years away from actually having sex with anyone, I vowed that when I did, I would have incredible staying power and turn in the all-night performances spoken about in the lyrics of the R&B slow jams I heard on the radio. Imagine my embarrassment when the charitable woman who relieved me of my virginity told me that my sexual strategy was overlong and boring. The moral? While it's good not to be a "two-pump chump," a quick and dirty romp can be just the thing.

Safety first: *the condom moment*

Sexy ways to apply latex We've come a long way in society. Cars can be sleek—yet safe. Condom companies have done their job by creating a wider-than-ever variety of comfortable, ribbed, lubricated, ejaculation-delaying, and sensation-enhancing condoms. It's up to you to learn to creatively, confidently, and seductively bring the condom out of the package and into the game.

It's wise to keep a good number and variety of condoms around—latex and nonlatex; smooth and textured; lubricated and nonlubricated. Once you choose the condom that's right for you both, it's time to put it on in the sexiest way possible. Putting on a condom doesn't have to be a rushed, awkward affair. By incorporating it into the sex act seamlessly, you will be better situated for relaxed, comfortable, sexy sex. Ultimately, everyone has their own specific moves for putting on a condom. The key thing to remember is to get it on while keeping your heads in the game and staying fully focused on the amazing sex that you're about to have.

After you First, decide who's going to apply the condom. If you're uncomfortable doing so, get comfortable with it. Practice putting one on during masturbation if you're a guy or, if you're a woman, on a banana or dildo. Some men prefer it if their partner puts the condom on them, particularly if they are prone to going soft when the rubber meets the road.

Getting it on Once you decide who, the question is how. One doesn't have to put a condom on with one's mouth to make the application seductive. Although sliding a condom on using one's mouth is an option, it should only be done by those who have practiced and succeeded on their own, as teeth can puncture holes in condoms. We recommend using your hands—not your mouth—for this reason. Make sure to roll the condom down all the way to the base of the penis. Having a little extra condom at the base is common, as standard condoms are longer than most men's penises. If the condom doesn't reach the end of your penis, size up to a larger condom.

Women who are putting the condom on their guy would do well to compliment his penis throughout the process. Grab his penis and rub it before putting the condom on. Say "give me that cock" or "I can't wait to have you inside me" or whatever else is likely to make your vagina wetter and his penis harder.

Maintain the heat Keep kissing, touching, and groping throughout the process. If you take a break to put the condom on while stopping everything else that has to do with being naked, touching, or having sex, that changes the tone and makes everything about "getting it on" ("it" being the condom) rather than "getting it on" (this time, "it" being sex itself), which, for guys, can be a bit of a party pooper. This is why it can help if a man's partner takes charge of donning the condom, so that he can be free to soak up the sights, sounds, and tastes of sex while his penis is prepped for sex.

Helmet on Once the condom is on, rolled down, and free of air bubbles (squeeze any remaining ones out), men might find it fun to ask for a lick or a suck (again, as long as it's tooth-free). Then add water-based lubricant to the outside of the condom and the entrance to the ready-and-waiting vagina or anus. The act of rubbing lube up and down, up and down can also help perk up his erection if it's suffering from a momentary lapse of hardness. Even if the condom is prelubricated, keep in mind that it comes with very little lube. Water-based lubricant is quickly absorbed by the body, too, so don't worry about using too much. More is better at first. If it feels too slippery, give it a dozen or so thrusts and it should get better.

SAFE SEX CAN BE SEXY Today's condoms aren't just safer-sex devices (although, when used correctly, they do indeed greatly reduce the risk of pregnancy as well as STIs such as HIV, chlamydia, and gonorrhea). Rather, today's condoms are sexual-enhancement devices in their own right—sex toys, even. Consider this: my (Debby's) research team at the Center for Sexual Health Promotion at Indiana University found that, in a nationally representative study of Americans ages 14 to 94, sex with a condom was typically just as pleasurable, arousing, and orgasmic as without one. And for younger men and women, sex with a condom was sometimes even rated as more pleasurable, arousing, or orgasmic than sex without a condom.

Sure-thing positions

Orgasm-centric sex positions Just a brief glance through the *Kama Sutra* will make it clear that there is a mind-boggling number of positions for you to try out. As with ice cream flavors, each person has a handful of favorites, and what lights one person's fire may do nothing at all for someone else. But some positions seem to be universally popular, and for good reason.

Coital alignment technique The CAT is one of the few scientifically tested sex positions out there and it's been shown to help women learn to experience orgasm during vaginal intercourse with a man. Think of it as an adaptation of missionary, in which she's flat on her back with her knees bent and feet planted. In some versions, she wraps one or both legs around his legs or butt, but having her feet planted can give her more leverage. As for the

CAT is about *slow grinding,* using **his pubic area** to grind **against hers**

man, his shoulders should be positioned slightly past hers, closer to her ears. Rather than focused on thrusting in and out, CAT is about slow grinding, using his pubic area to grind against hers.

CAT is likely effective for many women for several reasons. It keeps stimulation firmly on a woman's clitoris, without giving and taking in the sometimes-frustrating way that in-and-out thrusting can do. By locking bodies together, women may be more prone to engage their pelvic floor muscles, which can enhance their arousal and ease of orgasm. It also allows for closeness, kissing, and talking during sex—all of which can be huge boosts for sexual pleasure.

Woman on top One of the most popular sex positions, this one gives her control over the angle of vaginal penetration. It's also a prime position for women who like to angle their bodies so as to target stimulation of their G-spot. If his penis bends forward, she might try leaning back to focus more of his bend on the front wall of her vagina. If his penis bends downward, she may want to try reverse cowgirl (by turning to face his feet) for G-spot play.

Woman on top is also an excellent choice if you get turned on by dominating him. Every move you make excites him a little more, so you can play with him to your heart's content.

When a woman is on top, her partner can also use his fingers to stimulate her clitoris or to reach out and finger her bum, enhancing pleasure for her and, let's face it, for him, too.

Doggie style Some people like it fast. And some like it dirty. While doggie style (also known as rear entry) doesn't have to be either fast or dirty, it's perfectly suited to both, for those who like it that way.

Doggie-style positions include "table style," with the receptive partner on all fours and with a flat back. It's also good for face-down-ass-up sex. Men who need a great deal of powerful thrusting to experience orgasm often thrive on doggie style, and it's ideal for women who want their hair pulled or crave the deep thrusting that few other positions can allow for.

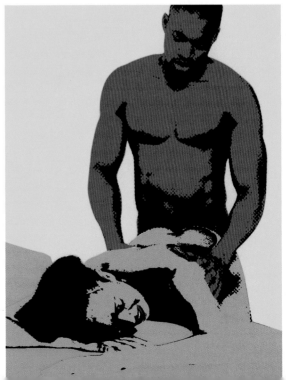

Soul-merging positions

Feel like you're really makin' love Sex can be a lot of things. Sometimes, it's pure, delicious filth—naughty, dirty, lots of fun. At other times, when you're with someone who's special to you, sex can be an expression of the tenderest feelings you have for each other. Certain positions set you up to feel so close to one another that you don't know where one of you ends and the other begins.

Good old-fashioned missionary It's the most popular sex position on the planet for a reason—and not just because it's easy. Missionary is physically comfortable for most men and women. The giver can be on top in a variety of formations—for example, lying on top of their partner or sitting on top with their hips at an angle that allows for more vigorous thrusting. Of course, when people are relaxed, they're more often able to reach orgasm—another reason why the ease of this position makes missionary king.

Missionary has many romantic possibilities, too, as it allows for lots of intimacy and kissing. And if there's a little light in the room, you can gaze into each other's eyes.

Scissors (face to face) In this version of the scissors position, face one another so that you can talk or whisper to each other. You can fondle each other's hair and brush against each other's cheeks and her breasts.

Get into this position by having each partner lie on their sides facing one another. The taker then opens her legs and scoots close enough to move the giver inside. This works best if the taker is well lubricated, naturally or with store-bought lube.

Another good version of the scissors position is for the giver to stand up at the edge of the bed while the taker sticks their legs straight up in the air and crosses them like scissors (thus tightening penetration). Although this variation positions you farther apart, it still allows for lingering face-to-face glances, thus heightening intimacy.

When relaxed you're *more able to reach orgasm,* which is why **missionary is king**

Spooning Many couples like to spoon together on a sofa while watching a movie or in bed as they drift off to sleep, and spooning can be an intimate position for making love. Although it's not face-to-face, the giver—in taking his partner from behind—can kiss his partner's neck and cheek during intercourse. The taker can reach back and take the giver's hand to kiss it, or to use it to massage their breasts or chest. Spooning is best suited to slow lovemaking, not for hard thrusts, and it's often a comfortable sex position throughout a woman's pregnancy as it doesn't put any weight on her stomach.

Pure *raunch*

Positions that feel gooood The following positions are often seen in porn because they're both visually interesting and more than a little risqué. They are also well worth trying out because they present a different range of angles at which the various bits and pieces interact. Save your Sade playlist for a more intimate occasion. These raunchy postures are best for when you're looking to ramp up the nastiness quotient.

Piledriver The name says it all and, as you can probably tell, it's not a position that's meant to engender emotional closeness. The receiver gets into a shoulder stand with their legs flipped over so the knees touch the floor on either side of their head, exposing their crotch. The giver kneels astride the taker's groin, takes their own weight in their arms, penetrates the taker and

The piledriver position will *cause the penis* to **rub into the G-spot**

positions their feet to enable them to move their hips as necessary. This position calls for the giver to angle his penis slightly downward into

the vagina or anus of the receptive partner. As erect penises tend to point somewhere between skyward and straight out at 90 degrees from the body, there is a bit of downward pressure. This "spring-loaded" feeling can be amazing, but don't push the erect penis too far beyond a comfortable range of motion. This position causes the head and ridge of the penis to rub into the G-spot of the vagina or prostate in men.

Knees to ears This is a raunchier variant of the missionary position, in which the receptive partner is effectively folded in half at the hips, their toes touching the floor above their head. The taker can hold their own legs with their hands or the giver can pin the taker's legs to the ground by putting some of their weight on the recipient's ankles. Not only does it make for deeper penetration and modified angle, the now-folded taker will be able to get a better view of the penis going in and out of them—a visual that a lot of people tend to like. If the taker is not quite flexible enough to achieve this

position, he or she can rest the backs of their calves or ankles on the taker's shoulders. Or, if he or she finds your feet a turn on, the taker will be well-placed to jam their little piggies in the giver's face as he or she pushes deep.

Prone bone This hot yet intimate position is like spooning (see page 119), except that the receiving partner is downward facing. You can start with the giver lying flat on top of the taker and explore several great variations from here. The taker can spread his or her legs, or close them tight, with the giver putting their legs on the outside of their partner's body. Now able to take his or her weight on the knees, the giver can be upright in a wide kneel, enabling them to spread, squeeze, slap, or simply admire the buttocks of the prone partner... or maybe even slide in a finger or thumb. Just because they are lying flat doesn't mean the receiving partner can't contribute to the fun: This is a great opportunity for them to slide one or both mitts under their body and take matters into their own hands.

You've-got-to-be-kidding positions

Ones you have to try at least once When you're old and feeble, sitting in the nursing home with dribble trickling down your chin, and sex is nothing more than a few—or hopefully a lot of—very happy memories, it's spectacular positions such as these that you are likely to recall most vividly. You'll also marvel at how fit and flexible you once were.

The armchair Upper body strength is a must for this position—and for both partners (you knew those push-ups and triceps extensions would pay off one day). The giver starts by leaning back and sitting on their butt, legs stretched out. The lucky receiver gets into position by sitting on their partner's lap, leaning back on their hands, and then slowly pulling one leg, then the other, up into place on either side of their partner's head. This tends to be a

slower-paced position and one that gives the receiver (on top) a good deal of leverage to move up and down, and back and forth (strength and flexibility permitting).

Standing wheelbarrow Think of it as a field day for adults! In this position, the giver has to be strong and steady as he or she stands up and holds the weight of their partner's body in their hands. After all, the taker will be supporting themselves only with the palms of their hands, with the rest of their body lifted in the air and their legs held by the giver, who is busy giving and giving and giving. Standing

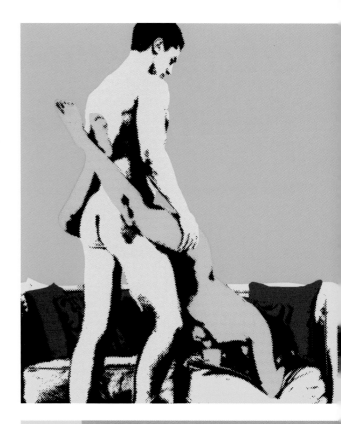

When considering standing wheelbarrow, think of it as a *field day* for **adults!**

wheelbarrow requires a lot of effort from both partners and thus isn't likely to be that orgasmic for either partner, but it can certainly be a fun memory for one's later years.

The airlift This is a game of trust in action, a position for which the giver has to be strong and confident to pull it off successfully. It begins with a leap of faith—and a leap into your partner's arms. That's right: Leap first, insert later (it's not terribly safe to leap onto a man's erect penis—or indeed to make quick, dramatic motions with one tucked inside you). Once you've been lifted up, kiss for a bit and then work together to get his Part A (penis, strap-on, etc.) into your Part B. Here, there's more potential for up-and-down movement than any other direction, with the giver using his hands to set the pace. An easy transition from this position is for the giver to move toward a hip-level dresser or work surface where the receiver can be placed, while the sex continues without additional pressure or strain to stay lifted midair.

Have-we-got-time-for-this? positions

Strip-and-go positions for when you're up against a tight deadline Work, kids, chores, and other commitments can conspire to cut down the amount of sex you have with your partner. It's easy to write this off as a mere bummer and fact of life, but a sustained dearth of sexy time can send your sexual chutzpah into a nose dive, resulting in even less playtime. Avoid this vicious cycle by snatching sex in stolen moments.

A little sumthin' In grown-up sex, snogging, hand jobs, blow jobs, and fingering are usually seen as warm-ups for the main event, but cast your mind back to when they were all ends unto

A **sex snack** tides you over until there's more time—and reminds your partner you're up for *a naughty bit of fun*

themselves. Get back into that teenage mind-set and treat each of these fun activities as individual units. A sex snack tides you over until you have more time—and reminds your partner that you're still up for a naughty bit of fun, and not just the person they traipse around the supermarket with on Saturday mornings.

Assume the position Quick sex is always aided by easy-access clothing: a short skirt that can be hiked up, a thong that can be pulled to

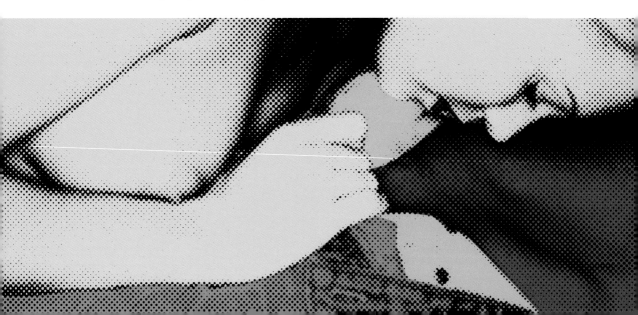

Freestanding sex works if the woman is wearing heels and tilts her pelvis back slightly. Plus, **sex in heels is hot!**

one side, a fly that can be easily breached. If you're attired this way, standing spoons—when the woman has her back to the man—can be done in a jiffy. Placing hands against the wall and legs apart like you're about to be frisked is very effective—especially if you have an authority fetish. This position is great for stuck elevators, supply closets, the changing rooms at the department store, etc.

Freestanding rear entry sex works well if the woman is wearing heels and tilts her pelvis back slightly. Plus, sex in heels is hot! You can also have standing sex face to face, though it may be a little trickier and demand a bit more physical strength. By tilting her pelvis forward, the female partner can make entry easier. Wrapping one or both of her legs around the male partner's waist can make for a more perfect union... provided he's been doing his squats at the gym.

Take a seat If you're pressed for time, say doing some important work or cooking an elaborate meal for your extended family who are all due to arrive any minute now, a great position is with the woman siting on a desk, table, or—if he's on the taller side—the kitchen countertop. With her skirt up and panties pulled to the side, all the gentleman has to do is stroll up and enter her while in a standing position. Couldn't be simpler.

This is a great quickie position, as being face to face still gives you the opportunity to furtively make out in the two to five minutes you've got before the phone rings, or your parents arrive for Sunday dinner. Don't burn the potatoes!

Yes, m'lady...

Getting in character If you played doctors and nurses as a kid, you've already participated in a sexual role-playing of sorts. You may not have known about sex itself, but you may have felt illicit excitement at having your privates prodded by a preadolescent GP or nurse. You and your contemporaries created a scenario where it was "okay" to have a look at the parts you didn't possess yourselves.

Well, the patient/doctor dynamic has a counterpart among grown-ups who want to tinker with roles, and it's just one of the countless personas people take on to create a context for different types of fun.

If you're completely new to the idea, this is going to feel a bit silly and requires surrendering your disbelief, which is harder than it sounds. For some people, dressing up lends the scenarios a greater intensity though some of the relationships outlined below don't actually require much in the way of costumes. Maybe start off with something less involved and work up to something more theatrical as required.

Bar pick-up scenario This is an easy starter role-play scenario. You arrange to meet at a bar, ideally an unfamilar one. One partner arrives earlier, perhaps wearing something the other hasn't seen before. The late-arriving partner shows up and, after making some fleeting eye contact, saunters over and embarks on some small talk. From here you can take it anywhere you like. Perhaps you're trying to recreate the thrill of the chase in which one of you is playing hard to get and it's up to the other to pull out every trick in the book to get them home. When you do, stay in character and resist doing the things you ordinarily would. This role play enables you to become different people, or at least allows you to play up a

start off with something **less involved** and work up to something *more theatrical* as required

certain aspect of your personality. It will also evoke memories of the exciting time when you first met your partner.

Master and slave This one entails one partner surrendering free will to the other and doing whatever he or she is told. If there is a naturally dominant partner in the relationship, it might be especially interesting if they become the submissive partner in the role play. Clients of

IF YOU STILL NEED CONVINCING
Consider this—it is much easier to lose your inhibitions when you are pretending to be someone else. In this way, role play can be a gateway into sex play you might not otherwise try. For example, spanking might not normally be high on your agenda, but it is almost a requisite part of the teacher/student scenario. Role play is also a great way to spice up the sex lives of couples as it allows you to try out different dynamics within the relationship.

S&M dungeons aren't generally janitors and sanitation workers. They're often high-level executives who hold a great deal of power over others. Being humiliated, helpless, and subservient to another person is completely alien to their day-to-day life and thus has a lot of erotic power for them. Many people respond strongly to being in either a dominant or submissive role. Start off gently with one partner doing whatever the other requests and see which role has a greater effect on you. As you get into more involved slave/master role play, remember to agree on a safe word (See Bound by love pp.138-139).

role play enables you to become **different people** or to play up different aspects of *your personality*

Teacher and student A classic dynamic in which the student is subservient to the older teacher. Teacher/student role play could involve the student being caught and reprimanded for some fitting infraction, such as skipping class or passing notes. Punishment could be meted out by the teacher putting the student over his or her knee and administering a spanking. Faced with detention, the student could offer the teacher a sexual favor in a plea for leniency.

Escort/client One of you texts a hotel name and room number to the other. At the hotel the "client" is greeted by the "escort," who informs them of the list of services. The client says what he wants and the agreed-upon fee is left on the table. In this setup, the scenario makes it okay for one partner to say in no uncertain terms what he or she is looking for and okay for the person playing the escort to either grant, deny, or put a price tag on his or her request.

If there's one thing I've learned about sex, it's that everyone is different. No one's physical or inner sex life can be guessed by what they look like or do for a living. Make your sex life your own by being honest with your partner, and it's likely to be good.

*"I would **never** have thought that he'd be **into bondage**. I'm so glad I brought it up—and I think **he is, too!**"*

she thinks...

Although men and women are more similar than they are different, more men tend to be down with kinkier sex. More men than women like to cross-dress, peep on others, or show off their stuff. It could be because women have more opportunities to be exhibitionistic as they go through their days—women can wear low-cut tops or skimpy bikinis whereas men are stuck in suits and shorts.

Women are often raised to equate sexual adventure with perversion, which isn't always the case. Men who would like to bring the kink out in their female partners would be wise to frame their interests as pleasurable exploration, rather than something to be ashamed of.

*"He would admire **my feet** and gently massage them—I couldn't help but be flattered"*

*"I was never into **talking dirty** until he coaxed me into trying it. He made me see how exciting it could be to **lose your inhibitions** like that"*

Women often worry that their partner's kinky interests mean that they're not sexy or wild enough on their own. Letting your partner know that you've long had this interest and that it makes your sex life better can show her a new side to kink.

"I dated a girl for 18 months before I told her that I wanted to bring another person into our bed. Imagine my relief when she told me that it was her number one fantasy, too"

Let him know that you are totally open-minded and nonjudgmental about any kinks or fantasies he has. Creating a feeling of trust—even in a short-term, physical fling—can make sex more unrestrained and fun.

I have to hold my hands up and admit that I'm a man of relatively simple tastes, but I've had lots of fun playing a part in other people's fantasies. I love being let into someone else's dirty mind.

"I knew a girl who loved being tied up. The idea itself wasn't a turn-on for me but *seeing how hot it got her* definitely was"

he thinks ...

"She leaned over and told me exactly **what she wanted to do to me** later—it was an instant turn-on"

Be proud of your kinks! Speak of your spanking interest as if it's something you're excited to share rather than worried he'll reject, and he might just be into it, too.

Too many people—men and women—think that kinky fantasies are something shameful and private best kept to the confines of Internet chat rooms. So ingrained is this tendency to hide and deny that many of us aren't even fully aware of our own fantasies. It's worth spending some time, then, figuring out what would really turn you on. And if you're feeling brave, let your partner in on it, too.

Tantric *teasers*

Give each other a surge of erotic energy Tantric sex, as described in the West, is different from Eastern spiritual Tantric practice. The two are often erroneously conflated, and we certainly don't intend to do that here. However, several of the ideas that have come from Western interpretations of Tantra can make for better sex. Below are a few we feel are particularly good to learn from.

Incorporate rituals Use ritual to mark sex as a special and important event, rather than just another thing that happens during the day. Some couples begin sex by removing their clothes and sharing a glass of wine. Others take a bath together and sensuously clean one another. Common rituals include decorating the "sex space" with flowers or candles, playing music as a way to begin, or embracing for several minutes before beginning your chosen Tantric sex practices.

Look into each other's eyes It's one thing to glance up and catch your partner's gaze during sex. It's another experience entirely to sit cross legged in front of one another, with hands resting on one's knees, palms facing up, as you breathe deeply and gaze into each other's eyes for at least five or ten minutes.

As you move away from initial eye gazing and into other sexual practices, try making eye contact as often as possible throughout the sexual event—although make this a general intention rather than a hard-set rule.

Focus on erotic touch Although partners often touch each other during sex (sex isn't just a meeting of genitals!), it's often something that just "happens" and may not feel intentional. By focusing on sensual or erotic contact, partners can remind each other how good it feels to be

By **focusing on sensual and erotic touch,** partners can remind each other *how good it feels to be touched*

touched in many different ways and places. Take turns caressing each other's bodies. The receiver can ask their partner to touch them in a certain place (such as the back, chest, legs, clitoris, head of the penis, neck, thighs, etc.) or in a certain way (e.g., fast, slow, longingly, passionately, with love).

Expressing gratitude and appreciation to your partner for touching you, and allowing you to touch them, can add to the intimacy of this aspect of Western-inspired Tantric sex.

Take your time Making sex more leisurely is a common goal of Tantric sex practices, for which making mental, physical, and emotional space for sexual expression is important. By going slow, you may be able to extend your lovemaking sensations and better master your own—and influence your partner's—sexual responses. If either of you climaxes, try to maintain your connection, rather than see orgasm as an "end" to sex (this is particularly true for men's ejaculation, which is too often seen as the signal that sex is over).

Breathe deeply Bring awareness of your breath into your sexual sharing. Some couples enjoy synchronizing their breathing patterns— some Tantrics do this with one partner straddling the other, such as by sitting in their lap, facing one another, and "harmonizing" their breathing. For other couples, it is enough for each person to focus on their own breathing, to take long slow breaths, and to notice how their sexual responses (such as their feelings of arousal or ease of orgasm) are influenced by their breathing patterns.

Multiple orgasms for men Certainly there is more to Tantric sex practices than learning to alter men's orgasms, but in my work as a sex scientist and educator, I (Debby) have

Multiple orgasms for men is the single *most asked-about aspect* of Western-inspired Tantric sex practices

found that this is the single most asked-about aspect of Western-inspired Tantric sex. The idea is that men can learn to extend their pleasure by delaying ejaculation. Practicing Kegel exercises (see pp.42–43) may help men increase control over their sexual response. Then, while masturbating or having sex, men can squeeze their pelvic floor muscles when highly aroused as a way to keep from ejaculating. This can extend the overall time they experience pleasure, and some men feel that they are able to experience peaks of pleasure—orgasms, even—over and over again, before they choose to let themselves ejaculate. Like other aspects of sex, we know of men who greatly value these exercises as part of their sexual practices as well as men who have tried it and found it wasn't for them. To each his own.

Touching *base*

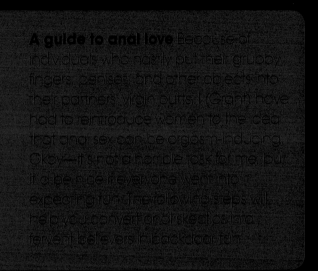

A guide to anal love Because of individuals who hastily put their grubby fingers, penises, and other objects into their partners' virgin butts, I (Grant) have had to reintroduce women to the idea that anal sex can be orgasm-inducing. Okay—it's not a horrible task for me, but it'd be nice if everyone went into it expecting fun. The following steps will help you convert anal skeptics into fervent believers in backdoor fun.

Sort out the plumbing (Almost) nobody wants to think about poop during a sex act but, you know, shit happens. The first step to ensuring nothing yucky happens when your backyard's being explored is eating right and staying regular. This boils down to eating a lot of fiber and drinking plenty of water. If you're confident that your butt is debris free, you'll be more inclined to relax and concentrate on how fun this oft-neglected neighborhood can be.

Squeaky clean The next bit of prep takes place in the shower. Don't be shy about getting your soapy fingers right up in there to ensure that your rectum's spick and span. Not only will this make your adorable balloon-tie a pleasure to be around; it will also get you used to having stuff going in and out of there. Guys, the added bonus of spending some alone time with your fingers up your butt is that you're likely to become acquainted with your prostate gland.

Giving the attention Okay, so now that you're clean as a whistle, you're ready to expand the possibilities of sexual gratification. But first, let's imagine that you're the one administering the attention. When you're performing oral sex on either a man or woman, start caressing the buttocks and gently tracing your fingers along the crack, then around the starfish. If he or she is not climbing the walls, proceed with the lubed pad of your index or middle finger. Gently apply pressure and work your finger in a tiny circle. After you've... ahem... taken the temperature of the situation, gently slip your finger in farther until just the tip of your digit is in, then a tiny bit more, then up to your first knuckle, and so on. If you're not certain it's appreciated, ask, "Does that feel good?" If it's a new area for them, keep lines of communication open. You might both find that having a finger in their butt hastens their orgasm or makes it more powerful. Or it might make it difficult for them to get off.

Getting stuck in So if you've had fun with all that, you might think about giving or receiving a penis or penis-sized/shaped toy. Relaxing and taking deep breaths is key for the receiver. If they are not an old hand at anal sex, lube is a good idea. Don't be stingy with it. A well-lubed insertion is going to help produce that good, smooth, gliding feeling. You can apply lube to the penis, to the sphincter, or preferably both.

Make sure you let the receptive partner be in control of the speed and depth of insertion at first. The best method here is for the "pitcher" to make like a statue and the "catcher" to back that ass up or lower it onto an erect penis or toy. Getting used to the sensation can take a while, so it's important for the penis owner to stay stimulated, lest things get bendy at the pivotal moment. The receptive partner can take charge of the action until he or she knows what they're comfortable with.

Once comfortable with the basic sensation, you can experiment with different anal-sex positions. The most popular is the anal variant of "doggy style." Some people find a modified missionary position, with the knees pulled up toward the chest, more comfortable. You can also have anal sex in a spoons position or with the receptive partner on top, giving them control.

Anilingus Giving and/or receiving oral anal attention is super fun. It's not gender specific (everybody's got one, to quote an old saying) so it's just about the most egalitarian thing you can do in the bedroom. Incidentally, performing/receiving anilingus is possible in a 69 position.

Because of the area's primary function, there is an increased risk of contracting hepatitis A, B, and C along with a range of other ailments. Many medical professionals recommend using a dental dam as it is the only way to prevent against getting something nasty, although you can also reduce some of the risks associated with licking ass by keeping your hepatitis A and B vaccinations up to date.

"anal sex is definitely one of my favorite things, but I can't imagine Julie Andrews singing about it"

Toy *story*

Battery-powered buzzes Sex toys, once highly taboo items, are now more mainstream than ever before, with an increasing number of couple-friendly sex boutiques dotting city and neighborhood streets worldwide, all sporting a mind-boggling choice of ingenious gadgets designed with pleasure in mind. Toys are in, and couples can have a lot of fun playing together.

Good vibrations Couples who are new to each other and to sex toys might add a little spice to their safer sex lives by reaching for a condom with a vibrating ring. The ring straps on to the man's penis, turning his genitals into a living sex toy. Most are single use and low- to moderate-intensity, making them ideal for beginners. Couples who no longer use condoms can still get in on the fun by using a vibrating cock ring, sold at many home sex-toy parties and in sex shops. Look for one with multiple speed and pulse patterns.

Vibrators are very popular among couples (see box). There are many, many types to choose from, with different styles designed to stimulate you in different ways. For example, there are special G-spot vibrators, vibrators designed for clitoral stimulation, rabbits, dildos, egg-shaped vibrators... the list goes on. Some sex toys are designed to be worn during intercourse. These are often U-shaped, with one of the branches meant for insertion into the vagina or anus. The inserted branch is relatively thin, which leaves plenty of room for all but the thickest of men to let their penis join the party, too.

Of course, the toy itself doesn't have to be couple-specific in its design or marketing to make sex more fun together. Anything that you can use alone can also be used with an open-minded and willing partner. A vibrator of any size can be applied to a female partner's

The vibrating condom ring *straps onto the man's penis,* turning his genitals into **a living sex toy**

clitoris during foreplay or intercourse, although smaller-sized vibrators, especially those designed for external stimulation, are easier to position in between two bodies. Opt for a multispeed dial if you're sharing a toy with a partner, just in case you prefer different intensities (which is sometimes the case). Women often want more and more power. Men, however, may find that

VIBRATORS FOR COUPLES A few years ago, my (Debby's) research team at Indiana University conducted a large-scale national study of vibrator use in the United States. They found that 53 percent of women and nearly half of men had used a vibrator (most of men's use was with a girlfriend or wife, but nearly one in five men said they'd used a vibrator alone as well). Also, most men weren't at all threatened about women's vibrator use. In fact, they were very supportive of it—and women themselves were similarly on board with the idea that vibrator use can be a healthy part of a couple's sex life.

sky-high intensity prompts them to come more quickly than they'd like (in which case, different settings can be valuable).

Strapping it on Many couples are curious about strap-ons. There are various types to choose from, with many different features. Some strap-ons consist of a harness for which you can get an insertable dildo. If you find a harness you like, ask the sex shop assistant to recommend a dildo that will fit well into the harness, as you'll want one that will stay snugly in place during use.

Also, some harnesses have a space for a small vibrator so that the strap-on wearer can get off on vibrations while the receiving partner gets pleasure from, you know, receiving.

Strap-ons can be used by couples of any gender combination: two women, two men, or man and woman. They can be huge or standard sized. The harnesses may be waterproof or not, and some come in adjustable sizes, so make sure to do your homework and ask for the options that are important to you before you buy.

Sensible precautions Before you share a sex toy with a partner, make sure that you've both been tested for STIs, have been treated for anything you need or want treatment for, and that you're comfortable with each other's STI status and understand what it means for you as sex partners. Sex toys can carry organisms along for the ride, something that women who have sex with women are often very familiar with and cautious about. To reduce the risk of sharing bacterial or viral infections, make sure you clean sex toys before and after every use. Slip a condom over a vibrator or dildo that's going to be shared. And by all means, keep an open mind! Sex-toy play alone can be great fun—and with a partner, even more so.

A touch *of kink*

Whips, clamps, crops, and paddles There are many BDSM toys to choose from (BDSM comes from the terms bondage and discipline, dominance and submission, and sadism and masochism). If you find such kinks intriguing, there's plenty for you to explore, but keep in mind that the central tenet that drives all BDSM play is that it is safe, sane, and consensual.

As far as being consensual goes, this isn't just about consenting to have sex or not. It is a detailed process that includes making sure you're using toys or props that are acceptable to everyone involved. This means that you should only buy a whip that the person being whipped is into—not one too light, and certainly not one that's likely to deliver more pain or discomfort than they've signed up for. Beginners would be wise to shop for props together. Those who are more into BDSM might find it helpful to add some detail about toy shopping and use in their master-slave contract, if they have one. And, of course, if you have questions about your or your partner's physical health and safety, and how it relates to using these kinds of products, please take your questions to a sex-positive healthcare provider.

Here are a few basics to consider for each of the following types of prop.

Whips These come in a range of materials, including latex, rubber, leather, suede, and nylon. Shorter whips are often recommended for beginners, as they allow for better aim and control. Only go for larger 12 inch, 18 inch, or longer whips once you're more seasoned and can really aim your strokes. Note, too, that there are certain areas that are okay "whipping zones" (such as the fleshy part of the butt, the upper back, and the legs), while some others

Clamps can be left in place rather than constantly having to **squeeze a nipple, lip, or vaginal lip**

are generally not safe to whip (such as the neck, face, head, and lower back near to where the kidneys are).

To practice your aim, start by whipping a pillow rather than your partner. To get a sense of how the whip feels, practice on the inside of your own arm. Whips don't even have to be used for actual whipping per se—the tails of the whip can also be dragged softly over your partner's body.

If you're new to whipping, you might see if a sex shop or club in your community—or at your favorite vacation spot, where you're unlikely to run into neighbors—offers beginners' workshops. Often these classes give men and women the chance to get firsthand experience trying out toys, all while learning how to safely give and receive pleasure.

Crops These are kind of like whips, but they often have an end to them that's more like a paddle. The paddle can be used to "train" a submissive partner to do the things you want them to do, to redirect them according to where and how you want them to move, or to slap them on their thighs to spread their legs wider for you. Crops generally offer greater control than a whip, so they may be good for beginners—as long as you've agreed on your boundaries in advance, as should be true for all BDSM play.

Paddles These are common tools for spanking. They, too, come in a range of materials including wood and plastic. They may also be covered with leather or with something soft, such as cotton or fleece. Paddles tend to have a larger surface area, so they can be used to spank more of a person's body, such as an entire butt cheek, or the area where the butt meets the thighs. Although sex paddles can be purchased in many sex shops and online, you can also use the back of a hairbrush or a kitchen spatula in a pinch.

Clamps Clamps may be vibrating or nonvibrating, and some people use just basic clothespins. Mostly, clamps are used on the breasts. However, some people clamp women's labia and parts of men's genitals, too. Clamps have sometimes been described as the "lazy kinkster's best friend" as they can be fixed on and left in place rather than constantly having to squeeze a nipple, lip, or vaginal lip. Some people clamp the insides of a partner's arm. Others clamp the outside of the breast, placing clamps or clothespin–s in a circle. The buttocks can be clamped as can the legs or other body parts. Have fun exploring! Sometimes the least-expected place to clamp feels the best during the clamping, or during the release.

Always respect your partner's comfort zone and boundaries. Don't leave clamps on for long amounts of time and remove the clamps if they cause serious discomfort, bruising, or restrict their blood flow.

Bound by *love*

Why tying, strapping, binding, and cuffing is sexy Most people don't tie each other up during sex with any frequency, but that doesn't mean it's not a central or exciting part of sex for some. It absolutely is. And if you fall into the category of people who have never tried restaining their partner as a part of sex play, we say read on. You might just be inspired to try something new the next time the opportunity arises.

People have different reasons for liking or being aroused by playing with tying, binding, gagging, or cuffing. Some people say they enjoy the intricate and creative ways in which being tied up forces them to play together. Others like the idea of tying a partner up, not because they want their partner immobilized, but because they want to rescue them. And, of course, some people like being tied and bound because they feel like they can leave all their responsibilities behind and surrender to release, relaxation, and pleasure. In that way, it's sort of like taking a trip to one of the few islands left on the planet that doesn't have Internet access—you can forget all about the world and just be where you are in the moment.

Pick your binding partner with care
If you want to be bound or tied, be careful who you tell about this fantasy. It's a tough thing to say, but the fact is that some people will take advantage of a woman or man who asks, let alone begs, to be tied up.

If you're new to binding and tying, it may seem like a romantic or sexy fantasy to have a partner creatively make knot after knot to restrain you. Maybe they leave you there for a while, telling you what they want to do to you. And maybe they actually do quite a lot of these very sexy, scandalous things. This can be a very rewarding scene between two partners who know and trust each other well. In the hands of someone who's unkind or worse, it can spell total disaster.

Kinky friends
If you're just getting into BDSM (bondage/discipline, dominance/submission, sadism/masochism) play, we think it's worth connecting with your local BDSM community. Many towns, large and small, have active BDSM communities. Some meet weekly or monthly over lunch, dinner, or film screenings to talk about their interests, share stories, and to welcome and educate new members about the lifestyle. Some kinksters are quite generous with their time and offer to hold beginner's workshops on topics such as rope play, handcuffing, safe fire play, or flogging.

Signing up for a workshop at a community space where you feel comfortable can be a good way to get into BDSM. Also, some sex shops and boutiques offer their own workshops so not only can you learn the skills needed for safer BDSM play, but you can also leave with products in hand that will help you make your sex dreams a sexy reality—products such as nylon rope, quick-release handcuffs, soy candles that make for safer sex-play dripping, and/or clamps and gags.

"Padded handcuffs are *great for beginners—* comfortable and there's no need to untie knots. Just don't lose the key!"

Establish a safe word One of the most important aspects of BDSM play is having a safe word that signals to your partner to play more gently or to stop altogether. Because saying "no," "stop," or "that hurts" is often part of the way people play together, these aren't good safe words or phrases. Some couples choose words that they are unlikely to ever use as part of sex, such as "tomato" or "rabbit." Others skip words altogether and use a little device that has a button they can press to shine a light that means stop. This is especially key if you're being bound and gagged and might not be able to utter your safe word—as long as you can press a button to shine your stop light, you're in better shape to make room for the parts of your sex play that you do want, crave, and enjoy with each new scrumptious knot.

The more, *the merrier*

Threesomes, foursomes, and moresomes Group sex has been famously depicted in the art of the ancient Greeks and Romans, but the human desire to get down with multiple partners almost certainly predates the orgies of our toga-wearing forebears. In fact, the word "orgy" means "secret worship," which refers to the use of group sex in pagan religious ceremonies. Nowadays, many people still like to spread the love.

Threesomes There are a few ways in which this can go down: You're in a relationship and inviting in a third, you've been invited to join a couple as a "guest star," or you and a couple of like-minded friends have decided to get to know each other better. Whatever the set up, the golden rule is that everyone must be equally enthused about the idea. If you're in a couple and get the sense that your whim is being indulged with anything less then unbridled gusto, it's time to weigh up whether living out your fantasy is worth potential aggravation later. If you're the one dragging his or her heels, make it known that you have reservations.

Beyond insisting on condom use, there's not much need to impose or conform to guidelines in such an otherwise freestyle activity. "No holes barred" is our take—but for some, the act of making something verboten offers a modicum of control, a nod to the sanctity and integrity of the relationship. Discuss your terms—if you need any—before you start the wheels turning.

Trust us on this: You're going to want to play with the third person a lot when you and your partner invite someone into your bed. But you'd be wise to divvy up your attention between them equally or even give your main squeeze the lion's share of the loving. Sexual jealousy can pop up without warning in group-sex situations. Making the experience inclusive for all may mitigate against it. If you're in the coveted "guest star"

A threesome is a *fantastic environment* in which to humor any **bi-curiosities**

role, you have less invested in the experience and will be getting the bulk of the attention. You're the novelty, the plaything. Enjoy it.

Being in close proximity to another gent's turgid chopper is a little too much for some heterosexual men, but the mathematics and mechanics of a male/male/female ratio can be more logical and transgressive than the expected male/female/female setup, adding to the excitement. Whether you're male or female, a threesome is a fantastic environment in which to humor any bi-curiosities you have.

GROUP SEX IN NATURE We need only look at our animal cousins to see that **group sex play has universal appeal.** The red-sided garter snake, for example, mates by having massive orgies with up to 25,000 participants. Unfortunately, the male snakes pile themselves on top of each other trying to reach breeding females and end up crushing the female participants to death. So, you know, try to avoid doing that.

Foursomes With foursomes, the setup is a little more symmetrical and, if everything is set up just right, egalitarian. The way this usually happens is that two couples decide to join forces. It's often the case that one half of a couple likes his or her opposite number slightly more than the other does. Being on either end of that equation can be super awkward! A perfect quartet is when you're each thrilled to bits with your temporary play partners and no one's... um... getting the shaft.

With a four, you've also got more options: You can be part of one eight-legged chimera, or watch your significant other get roughly plowed as you do the same to your play partner, or you watch the three of them go at it while you take a break to replace your electrolytes. Again, circumventing feelings of jealousy is key here. You really do have to be secure in your own attributes—sexual or otherwise—to be able to share the apple of your eye. If you can reason your way through those uncomfortable feelings and take pleasure in seeing your partner being sexual with others, the payoff may very well be worth it.

Moresomes If you're blessed with attractive, fit, vivacious, open-minded friends whom you know well enough to float the idea without them defriending you on Facebook, good for you! If you aren't or would prefer to keep it anonymous, there are many sex parties going on and a cursory Internet search should give you plenty to choose from in your area. Some of them are casual and free; others have a vetting process and charge a membership fee and/or cover charge. This is definitely an instance in which you get what you pay for. If you have a come-one-come-all policy toward the people you bump uglies with, go for it. If you're a bit more picky about the guest list, do your research and try and track down a soirée with a rigorously policed velvet-rope policy.

their charms, premature ejaculation is an explosive validation of them. If you do jump the gun on a first or early sex session, you could say something jovial and disarming like "Now that wouldn't have happened if you hadn't insisted on being so sexy." The average refractory period (the amount of time between having an orgasm and the ability to achieve another erection) is about 30 minutes[1]. Keep the conversation light and/or pay her some more attention and you should be ready to rock out with your cock out and restore her faith in your abilities in short order.

While many men get "crept up on" now and then, there are exercises dudes can try to develop ejaculatory control (see Jacking off, pp.58-59). Master them and you'll be a step closer to being a master in the bedroom.

Popping off early is **less likely to be taken poorly** than a floppy cock

Breaks and mistakes If your condom breaks during intercourse, you have to let your partner know immediately. Even though you did the right thing by using condoms, your chances of parenthood and contracting or spreading an STI just skyrocketed.

Best practice would be to both get tested and, if there's no other birth control method being used, to acquire the morning after pill. Hatching a plan about all this may very well have put the kibosh on your sexy evening, but if you do possess the steel to soldier through, don't forgo using condoms under the assumption that "the toothpaste is out of the tube." There's a good chance that it isn't. By finishing how you started, you're being a responsible citizen, which speaks volumes about your respect for your partner and yourself.

From "ow" to "wow"

When sex is uncomfortable Here's a shocking fact: 30 percent of women ages 18 to 59 report having some degree of difficulty with pain during the last time they had sex, compared to about five percent of men[1]—an astounding gap. Women and men are likely to experience discomfort for a number of reasons, some having to do with medical issues, others as a result of inexperience or freak accidents.

Although there's no way to prepare for every eventuality—and you certainly can't rule out the possibility of accidental mishaps—there are some things you can do to make sure sex is as comfortable as possible for all parties. Here are a few things to keep in mind to keep things going more or less as they should:

Warm up If you've got a bit of time and this isn't a quickie situation, try to spend at least 10 or 15 minutes doing fun, sexy, arousing things before any kind of vaginal penetration happens. This allows natural vaginal lubrication to kick in and the vagina to "tent," which means it gets bigger when aroused (this is a good thing, as it makes more room for fingers, sex toys, or a penis).

Keep lube on hand This should be water-based lubricant, preferably, as it goes with a wider range of sex toys, condoms, and birth control methods than any other lube. Not only will it make everything more comfortable; using lube will also greatly reduce the risk of vaginal bleeding. If sex is mostly uncomfortable at the point of entry, lube both partners' parts up with a dab of lube the size of a coin.

Stay flexible You'll be much better suited to move into comfortable sex positions, and out of painful ones, if you're fit, active, and flexible.

HE SAYS A friend of mine broke his penis during sex. That's right: He actually fractured his penis. A rather zaftig casual sex partner was on top of him, facing his feet—a position you may know as reverse cowgirl—when he slipped out and her weight came down directly on top of his erection. He heard a popping sound and felt a wetness on his thighs, but initially felt no pain, so thought that his partner was the hemorrhaging party. Then he felt a rush of pain and took off the condom. Before passing out he saw jets of blood shooting from his penis and onto the walls of his partner's parents' basement. He eventually came to on a helicopter en route to New Jersey's number one penile reconstructive surgeon. By this point, he'd lost almost three pints of blood. It turned out that his urethra had broken and the corpus cavernosum—the spongy tissue that fills with blood when a man is aroused, creating an erection—emptied out all over the place.

I'll spare you the more grizzly details but suffice it to say that his penis got taken apart, fixed up, and put back together again. He had sex again within two months of the accident—albeit gingerly—and, before the year was out, had sex with the partner he'd been in the accident with. Closure indeed. I'm telling you this because, immediately after it happened, he told me to tell as many people as I could that this is even a possibility so that they could guard against it. You have been warned.

Go slow At least at first. Bodies change on a daily basis, especially women's vaginas, which are always in flux thanks to the menstrual cycle. Starting off slow gives both partners a chance to figure out how things feel today and whether they feel ready to rumble or more into cuddly sex.

Say "ow!" When it hurts, speak up. Don't expect a grimaced look on your face to communicate for you. For one, it may be dark. Also, everyone's "O" face is a little different and your partner may think you're loving it when really you're hating it. Say something and, yes, "get off me" counts. If it hurts, it should stop. You can always try again later.

starting off slow gives you a chance to figure out whether you feel *ready to rumble* or more into cuddly sex

Take care Be aware of where your body is in relation to your partner's—and mindful of their specific sensitivies. Men's testicles are notoriously sensitive, so it is advisable to keep knees and elbows out of their immediate vicinity. It is also possible, though very rare, for a man to break his penis. If you hear it "pop," stop everything—he needs to go to the doctor ASAP. Partners of women should be aware that vaginal tears are often the result of unlubricated or rough sex. Always make sure that your partner is ready before, ahem, plowing ahead.

Get ongoing pain checked out Not all painful sex is easily managed. If pain is ongoing, check in with a healthcare provider. It is possible that a condition needing medical attention may be at the root of the problem.

Rutting *in a rut?*

How to make over a lackluster sex life For most of us, sex within a relationship starts off with a flurry of incredibly long, frequent, innovative sessions before gradually tapering into something a little less intense, impassioned, spontaneous, and frequent. If you feel your sex life has become a bit of a snooze, the good news is that there are plenty of steps you can take to revitalize it.

Nighttime isn't necessarily the right time If the sex you have seems to coincide with evenings when there's nothing much on TV, you may need to make some simple changes, such as rearranging the schedule. Find that you're doing it on weekend nights? The next time you wake up before your partner, bring them around with your hot mouth around their parts. Don't think there's time to get down to it, when you've only got five minutes to spare? Pah-lease. A little bit of unexpected tomfoolery can go a long way to restoring some of that *je ne sais quoi* you thought was consigned to the past. Stealthily perform oral sex without a thought of reciprocation and you'll surprise your partner—and yourself—with how quickly the cobwebs can be brushed away.

Change the scenery If there's been a regular place for sex, we're guessing it's the bedroom, and we can see why—it's private, comfortable, familiar—but it's also where you sleep, resulting in the location informing the timing: when you're exhausted. (No wonder he's not busting out the Piledriver lately.) Next time you're having a cuddle in the living room, keep it there. Your surroundings alone will inform sexual positions and techniques that might not occur to you in bed. One partner is suddenly bracing him or herself against the coffee table, or using their sitting position to facilitate an exciting new posture. The shower can allow for a change (great for mornings), or

Think there's no time when you've only got five minutes? *Pah-lease.* A **little bit of tomfoolery** goes a long way

even try the kitchen, in which countertops and tables offer many possibilities. If you're feeling adventurous, you can fool around outside the house. Roughly hump your loved one against a tree on a woodland walk, or consider a changing room in a clothing store. "How does my butt look in these jeans, darling?" "Good enough to eat. Now take them off!"

BREAK THE ROUTINE We've spent a lot of space in the last few chapters talking about the importance of foreplay, but you'll notice that we've never outlined a particular sequence. That's because **there doesn't have to be one**. If you've been conforming to kissing, groping, hand job, fingering, cunnilingus, missionary, doggie, her on top, and then lights out, it's hardly surprising that your sex life is lacking sparkle. Try playing with the sequence of events. You might find that eschewing something that's worked well in the past results in finding something that works so much better.

Porn and toys Bringing external stimuli into your sex life is great for adding some missing flair. Tell your partner to find three porn clips that really turn her or him on while you do the same. Then bring the laptop to bed and watch them together, explaining what it is about them that's captured your imagination so. You might surprise your partner (and yourself) with how you tick, and it's likely to get them thinking dirty thoughts about you once again.

Using toys is also a great way to start thinking differently about your sex life. Find a sex toy shop where the staff is knowledgable and helpful and surprise your partner with something to go

Different surroundings inform sexual techniques and positions that might not occur to you in bed

exploring with. Remember that there are an increasing number of sex toys on the market for men, too, so this impromptu gift can be for him.

Seeing other people This doesn't have to be the death knell of a relationship, but rather the start of a new chapter—if you keep your jealousy in check. You may find your passion for your partner is revivified by allowing them to be their sexual selves with others. Perhaps you could encourage them to flirt with someone at a bar, or make a list of celebrities they're permitted to sleep with. If you enjoy seeing your partner through someone else's eyes, kick it up a notch—put some hot body pictures of them on the Internet and enjoy the emails from voyeurs. If you're particularly secure in your relationship, you could give them a free pass to sleep with someone new, maybe on the proviso that it's a one-time thing only, and you get to hear all the details.

Chapter 7
Yes, yes, yesssss!

Her climax scene

The whys, hows, and whens of her orgasm A woman and her partner kiss fervently, the sound of music or the ocean in the distance. They tug at each other's clothes and tumble into a conveniently nearby bed where they roll around under soft white sheets. Very soon, her mouth is open, her eyes rolled back as she moans loudly in total, orgasmic ecstasy. This is, of course, a Hollywood movie—it's not real life.

Dispelling misinformation Many women grow up believing that sex and orgasms are in real life as they are portrayed in romance novels and films—easy, explosive, and reliable. Until, of course, they start having sex for themselves. Just as men absorb a great deal of misinformation about sex through watching porn, women are misled by romantic movies and novels. (Of course, we're all exposed to both porn and mainstream movies/novels but, generally, men are more exposed to porn, and women to stories about love and sex.) This matters because, when women start having sex, they often wonder what's wrong with them. When I (Debby) teach human sexuality classes to college students, her female students often ask her, "What's wrong with me? I can't have an orgasm!", while male students similarly approach her saying, "What's wrong with me? I can't give her an orgasm!"

Understanding the whys, hows, and whens of orgasm can help us all feel a little more relaxed about sex—and a great deal more confident about moving forward, ready to have fantastic sex rather than "What's wrong with me?" sex.

Some women aim for orgasm *because they feel it's their right,* and because it makes for **satisfying sex**

Let's start with the whys Over the past few decades, the female orgasm has become a more important part of sex. It used to be that fewer women felt an orgasm was necessary for satisfying sex. Now, more women are stepping forward to ask their partner to help with their orgasm and also to do it themselves. In part, women's activism in the 1960s and 1970s is owed a great deal for this shift, as it encouraged women to learn about their bodies, explore with masturbation, and teach themselves as well as their partners how to find their clitoris, touch their breasts, or move in and out of their vagina in ways that feel good. In part, then, some women aim for orgasm because they feel it's their right, and because it makes for satisfying sex. Having an orgasm is also important for many women because not only does it feel exciting, but it also seems to satisfy their partner who may be putting in a great deal of effort

THE EMOTION OF ORGASM Having an orgasm can help people feel emotionally close to one another, perhaps in part due to **the release of oxytocin at the time of orgasm.** Oxytocin has been called the "cuddle hormone" and is thought to have a role in pair bonding, although more research is needed to understand its role in human relationships.

and frequently asking, "Did you come?" (this is also why many women fake—to silence and satisfy an overeager or insecure partner).

As for the hows We know that the majority of women are capable of having orgasms, and most seem able to orgasm during vaginal intercourse—although it may take practice, patience, and perhaps some extra help in the form of a finger on her clitoris, a position that directs stimulation onto her glans clitoris or the front wall of her vagina, or a vibrator. Of course, women vary, and for some, spanking, dirty talk, or whispered words of romance and love may be more likely triggers of orgasm.

If she tells you what works for her, listen and give it a try. If she makes suggestions to tweak

About a third of women sweat a little and go *pink in the face and chest* (the so-called **"sex flush"**)

your technique, keep an open mind. Remember that everyone is different. What worked for your ex, or in a porn movie, might not work for her.

What about the whens? Most women take time to reach orgasm—and some rarely get there (which isn't always a problem—some just "enjoy the ride", so to speak). When it happens, though, orgasm tends to last around 20 or 30 seconds on average. Vaginal, uterine, and anal muscles contract. About a third of women sweat a little and some go pink in the face and chest (the so-called "sex flush"). Her orgasm may be silent or loud. She might laugh or cry, without meaning to, due to the emotional experience of orgasm. And when it happens, it's likely to be very, very good.

His climax scene

The whys, hows, and whens of his orgasm It's pretty safe to say that the male orgasm isn't nearly as ethereal as its female counterpart. But that's not to say that it's any less fascinating. The male orgasm is, in fact, a wonder of hydraulic engineering; a sequence of events begins, plateaus nicely, and then becomes almost impossible to stop. Here's how those stages take place.

The excitement phase This is underway when the penis starts to become partially erect, often after just a few seconds of stimulation, with the onset of blood rushing into the spongy tissue in the penis, called the corpus cavernosum. During an extended excitement phase, the erection may be partially lost and regained several times. Heart rate increases, as does the rate of breathing. It's all happening!

The plateau This is the period of sexual excitement prior to orgasm. The phase is characterized by increased circulation and heart rate, increased sexual pleasure with increased stimulation, and further increased muscle tension. This is the stage that many men, myself (Grant) included, like to drag out for as long as possible. Now, breathing continues at an elevated level. During this phase, the urethral sphincter contracts, so as to prevent urine from mixing with semen and to guard against retrograde ejaculation, and muscles at the base of the penis begin a steady rhythmic contraction. The testicles rise closer to the body.

The buildup When an orgasm is imminent, a man will notice an increase in the size of the head of his penis (his partner probably will, too), and it will turn extra purplish in color. Something called the Cowper's gland will start producing a clear fluid, commonly known as

The plateau is the *period of excitement* prior to orgasm, the stage men like to drag out **as long as possible**

"precum," which will start dribbling out of his urethra. His balls will swell and draw even closer into his body. His love gun is now, ahem, cocked. Around this point his face and chest may flush as he experiences increases in heart rate, blood pressure, and muscle tension. With extreme ejaculatory control this amazing feeling can be prolonged but, for most men, it represents "ejaculatory inevitability" or the famed "point of no return." Semen is now collecting in a pool at the base of his penis and he'll begin to feel what's usually described as a tickling feeling followed by a throbbing sensation in his urethra. The wheels are in motion now. Look out!

Ejaculation Exactly when this happens in relation to the big O varies from man to man. Some men experience the orgasm several seconds before ejaculating; others ejaculate first, then experience *"la petite mort."* Still others experience them in concert. Contractions or pulses in the urethra, prostate, and perineum, spaced just under a second apart, push semen out of the penis. For some men this can shoot several feet at a speed of up to 43 miles per hour. For others, it simply dribbles out. How dramatic the ejaculation is depends on several factors, including the length of time that's passed since he last ejaculated, how toned his pelvic floor muscles are, and the size of his urethral opening (you know what happens when you squeeze the end of a garden hose). Semen usually comes out in three or four spurts that

With extreme control this *feeling can be prolonged* but, for most men, it represents **the point of no return**

correspond with the rhythmic contractions of his perineum. Once he's "spent," blood will flow out of the corpus cavernosum and his scrotum and testes will shrink down to their normal size and travel back to their normal location.

Refractory period The refractory period is the length of time after orgasm during which it's nearly impossible for the man to maintain his erection and ejaculate again. It's been referred to as the only period in a man's life when he's sated enough to not be thinking about sex for a few minutes. For teenagers this period of downtime can be as little as a few minutes. For men in their 70s, it may take a full 24 hours before they're recharged and ready to go. The average refractory period for men is around 30 minutes.

Ladies *first?*

Après vous Chivalry, they say, is dead. It sort of got forgotten about as traditionally held gender roles were dispensed with when it was suggested (over a long period of time) that they were a little silly. However, putting the needs of others, especially your sexual partners, first is most certainly not silly. But with simultaneous orgasms still a pipe dream for most, the question needs to be asked: Who should come first?

The theory In order to answer this question properly, we must first confront a few facts about the differences between men and women. Guys and gals can have very different sexual response profiles. Generally speaking, most men can go from floppy to finished in the time it takes water to boil, and when they do, they are usually out of the game for a while. His time out can be as little as a few minutes or as much as a day or so, the "refractory period" tending to get longer with age. Women on the other hand tend to achieve orgasm after a lengthier and sustained period of arousal and can continue having sex. They may even find that subsequent orgasms increase in intensity. The take-home message from these differences is that heterosexual couples should generally adopt a ladies-first policy to ensure that everybody is left satisfied.

Of course there are exceptions to this general rule. Some women climax incredibly quickly; some men take longer. Some women only like to orgasm once while there are some men who barely have a refractory period at all. The general aim is that both of you end up feeling happy with the outcome.

In my (Grant's) experience, once you've made a woman come at least once, any lingering performance anxiety melts away. Not only will it make you look incredibly generous, taking care of that first orgasm means that the pressure's off. By embracing and not bemoaning this difference in timing, you can turn your different arousal profiles into an asset.

Making it happen As we've mentioned throughout the book, a tried and tested way to bring her to a powerful orgasm is to not skimp on revving up her arousal with kissing, touching, fingering, oral sex, and maybe some choice verbalizing of what's going on in your dirty mind. If you've done all that and fear that you don't have the staying power to finish her off with penetrative sex, know this: Not all women climax through penetration alone. Even those who do generally like to experience orgasm when full to the brim, will also generally be happily orgasmic to the tune of fingers, tongues, toys, and other ways to play.

If lasting long enough worries you, here's your action plan to being chivalrous. Finger and go down on her until she has an orgasm. Make sure she knows that it's as fun for YOU as it is for HER with a series of moans and terse statements about how good she tastes. Once she's got one out of the way, then and only then think about putting your penis in. Unlike men, many women can have an orgasm hot on the heels of another. You could find that putting it

in after an oral orgasm makes the second, or even third, a piece of cake.

Another way to ensure that she gets off before you peter out is to encourage her to play with her clit as you slide in and out of her. Any position is good for this but doggie, spoons, and reverse cowgirl give her ample room to work.

And if you're one of those men who can last long enough to give orgasms to a roomful of women (lucky you—and them), edge all you want. Give her as many orgasms as she desires (if she's multiply orgasmic), checking in every now and then to see when she's had her fill. Even easily, multiply orgasmic women need to stop at some point so asking how she's doing or if she'd like another is kind of you—as is letting her know when you'd like to come.

The biggest mistake is for your orgasm to signal your sudden apathy to eliciting one from her. So you've made your O face. So what? Without missing a beat, get your mouth and fingers working down there and banish any thoughts of the sandman until she's screaming the place down. You might find her orgasm so arousing in and of itself that you're ready to go again. Huzzah!

> "He makes sure that I am **completely satisfied** first. I like to think of it as modern-day chivalry"

Plenty more *where that came from...*

Secrets of multiple orgasms Multiple orgasms are for greedy hedonists—and we mean that in the most complimentary of ways. It's no wonder that, having tasted the enormous pleasures of one orgasm, some people will ask for a second helping (or a third, fourth, fifth...). Are these multiply orgasmic folks orgasm gluttons? Absolutely—and why not? Our bodies are built for pleasure, so why not play with them?

Scientists have no idea how many people are capable of multiple orgasms. Most studies are conducted among small volunteer samples, and many people have never tried to have more than one orgasm, so they don't know if they could have multiple orgasms or not.

Regardless of how many other people have multiple orgasms, the real issue becomes how you and your partner can have more than one, if indeed that's what you both want.

For women If you've never had an orgasm, trying for one is the first step. If you have had orgasms before (even if just on occasion) and want to learn to have multiple orgasms, remember that arousal takes a long time to go away (often at least 10 minutes). If, after a woman has an orgasm, she feels she's lost arousal, she would be wise to toss that thought aside. Even if her thoughts have gone astray by thinking about work, school, or family stress, her body's genital arousal hasn't gone anywhere yet. By refocusing her thoughts on sex and pleasure, she can get in line with her still-aroused body and move in ways that feel good. This part is critical—it means that she should rely on herself rather than her partner's movements. She is the

She is the only one living inside her body, who can *feel all the tingles* and parts that are **screaming out for more**

only one living inside her body, who can feel all the tingles and warmth and parts that are screaming out for more. It's up to her to move her hips, to squeeze her pelvic floor muscles, to focus her fantasies on whatever sets her free to accept her next orgasm. When she finds something that feels good, she should go with it.

If your female partner is trying for another orgasm, pay attention to her and stay still if she's moving around your penis, fingers, or the sex toy you're sharing with her. And if she doesn't want another orgasm (or doesn't want an orgasm in the first place), try not to pressure her. Sometimes women feel tired, stressed, or like it's just not going to happen (or happen again) and that's okay. Also, some women who regularly have multiple orgasms know when one is particularly intense and may want to go out on a bang, rather than have their last one be just "so-so." Respect her orgasmic wishes.

For men Some people believe that it's not possible for men to have multiple orgasms. And in fact it is exceedingly rare for men to have multiple ejaculations, meaning that they have an orgasm (with ejaculation), stay erect, and keep having sex or masturbating, and then some time later have another orgasm (again, with ejaculation), and so on. There have been a few cases of such men, who seem hormonally different from most men.

That said, many men can teach themselves to experience multiple orgasms—it's just that they're orgasms without ejaculation, until the final one. Because ejaculation sets the refractory period into gear, avoiding ejaculation can keep men going without losing their erection.

Learning to experience orgasm's euphoric feelings without ejaculating is a challenge. Start by practicing edging techniques in masturbation (see Cool your jets, page 160), backing off when you are more and more aroused each time. Begin by backing off when you're about 60 percent excited, working up to backing off when you're 80 or 90 percent excited (when you

Some men find multiple orgasms a *significant boost* to their sex lives; others are satisfied with **one big bang**

may experience orgasmic feelings). Some men also try to back off by squeezing the pelvic floor muscles as they approach orgasm. Over time, with practice, squeezing your pelvic floor muscles can help prevent ejaculation while still making room for orgasm. Eventually you can ejaculate and call it a night. Some men find multiple orgasms a significant boost to their sex lives; others feel they're more work than they're worth and are satisfied with one big bang. Your call.

Squirms *and squirts*

Ejaculation tips for both men and women Believe it or not, ejaculation for guys is not always as straightforward as it seems. There are certain issues to consider, and these tips may help. But men are not the only ones who ejaculate. Some women do, too. Female ejaculation can be a fascinating source of sexual excitement and intrigue for the women who experience it as well as for their partners.

Female ejaculation With the popularity of Internet porn has come an increasing number of questions about how to "squirt"—in other words, how women can experience female ejaculation. But let's back up for a moment. It's important to state up front that scientists who study sex aren't entirely sure what to make of female ejaculation. Some don't even like the term "female ejaculation," as the fluids that come from a woman during sexual excitement or orgasm aren't the same as male ejaculation. It's almost as if we need an entirely new word to describe these fluids that are not semen, not vaginal lubrication, and certainly not urine.

Although some women feel as though the fluids are coming from the vagina, most scientific and anecdotal reports seem to suggest the fluids come from the urethra. Many women who experience female ejaculation stumbled upon it accidentally—it's just something that happened to them one day and that (hopefully) they and their partner enjoy.

Other women have taught themselves to experience female ejaculation by bearing down on their pelvic floor muscles during sex—a practice we don't recommend as it may weaken these very important muscles. Another way to try and experience female ejaculation is to simply open yourself to it. Sometimes women shy away from sexual stimulation that makes them feel as if they have to pee when, in fact,

it's extremely unlikely that a woman will actually pee during sex. Rather, those sensations may simply be nerve cross-talk (nerve endings get confused, too!) or they may be signs that female ejaculation is on its way. By relaxing into it and continuing with the types of stimulation that are getting her there, female ejaculation may occur. It can feel exciting, sexy, and impressive to see more fluid than usual come from a woman's genital area—but, like male ejaculation, female ejaculation can also be messy, so you may want have a towel ready. Or just grin and bear it, because sex is fun and unexpected like that.

Male ejaculation Men have diverse experiences related to ejaculation. Some men, probably about five percent or fewer, find it difficult to ejaculate, an experience that may be called delayed ejaculation (when it occurs after much trying) or inhibited ejaculation (when ejaculation doesn't happen, even after a great deal of effort). If you experience DE or IE, you'd be wise to check in with a healthcare provider to rule out any issues that may be getting in the way of ejaculation.

Assuming all is well in terms of your health, you may find it helpful to boost your mental and/or physical arousal. You might find it easier to ejaculate after you've primed yourself with porn, either during masturbation or sex with a

partner. Vibrating cock rings (sometimes sold as "condom rings" in drugstores and other mainstream venues) tend to provide a light-to-moderate intensity of vibration, and that may be enough to help you reach orgasm. However, vibrating cock rings available through adult bookstores and in-home sex toy parties may pack more punch and be easier tools to help get you off. More intense vibrators, such as wand-style vibrators, are sometimes needed to do the trick.

DE and IE can also have their roots in issues related to relationships, fear of letting go, or anxieties about impregnating a partner—for these and other reasons, seeing a sex therapist can be particularly helpful.

It can be *exciting, sexy, and impressive* to see **more fluid than usual** come from a woman's genital area

Then there are practical issues related to ejaculation. Figuring out where to ejaculate is important. If you're having vaginal or anal intercourse with a new partner, the answer may seem straightforward: Ejaculate in the condom, dummy! But she or he may prefer it if you wait to ejaculate until you remove your condom-covered penis from their vagina or anus—just to be sure. If you're lucky enough to be on the receiving end of oral sex, give a heads up that you're about to come so your partner can choose to take it in their mouth or let it flow into their hands or a nearby towel.

Finally, keep in mind that, with age, semen volume decreases, as does thrust and distance—but research suggests that you may delay these changes by staying fit and trim (around the waistline in particular), by not smoking, and by exercising your pelvic floor muscles.

Cool your *jets*

Tips for staying the course Guys: If you want to master anything you have to put in some serious practice. This goes double for mastering your sexual response. Soccer players hone their ball skills by doing kick-ups, musicians spend hours cranking out scales, and, if you want to be in complete control of when you unload, you could do a lot worse than working the "stop/start technique" in your free time.

1. Me time On an evening when you've got nothing else planned, block out some time for a session with yourself. Make yourself comfortable, start masturbating, and commit to being aware of what you're doing. Concentrate on the sensations you experience: what feels good, what you like, if you speed up, tighten your grip, if your breathing gets faster and shallower. Think about yourself as a study subject and get scientific with it.

2. In touch with yourself Without trying to prolong your session, as you approach orgasm just think about the feelings that you're experiencing. Many men usually describe it as a tickling sensation. Once you know what this feeling is like, you can begin to explore the sensations that take place directly before the "point of no return." During the next five times that you masturbate—over the next week or so—think about the sequence of events.

3. On the edge By now, you ought to have a good idea about the sensations preceding the tickle that signals your "sexy-time explosion." The next time you masturbate, simply let go of your penis as they occur. Leave yourself alone for about 15 seconds (or longer) and don't worry if your penis starts to soften a bit. Concentrate on the sensations that you feel as you take your foot off the gas. Once things have died down to a manageable level, slowly pick up where you left off.

4. Don't overshoot! Do this exercise again and again until you feel confident that you know when to let go. Each time, take notice of the feelings you're experiencing. When you're completely comfortable with it, try and take it a little bit further before you let go. This is called edging—you're working toward stimulating yourself to the very edge of coming and then stopping. By the way, this is fun to do regardless of whether you're trying to prolong your performance as it tends to make your eventual orgasm much more intense.

5. Endurance testing Make the edging toward orgasm and cooling off again part of your daily routine. It may be difficult at first: You may, ahem, overshoot the mark, you may lose your erection, you might even give yourself a severe chafing—but commit to staying the course. As you put in more time you'll notice that the "cool down" periods will decrease in duration while the stimulation periods will increase. You're making some serious progress! Try this stop-and-start method five to ten times in a session and fit in a session every day or two.

6. *Build it up slowly* Once you're more or less in control of your orgasm through this increased awareness of your sexual response, experiment with making your masturbation feel more like a mouth, vagina, or anus. Use a quality lube, use a tighter grip, or even a product like the Fleshlight, a sex toy for men that more closely resembles the various places you'll be wanting to put your penis. You can even begin to increase your mental stimulation by watching some of your favorite porn as you go through your stop-and-start routine. Once you can stop and start your session with comfort it's time to try it with a partner.

7. *Try it out* If you are in a relationship, you can let your partner in on how you've been stepping up your game and he or she will certainly be up for helping you out with the project when you take the time to explain the regimen. If you're testing it out with a new partner, don't get psyched out. You'll now be in control of the sequence of events that trigger your orgasm. When you feel it happening, slow down and stop the stimulation if need be. There's no need to stop the action completely however. Instead, use the cool down period to lavish some attention on your partner. They don't need to know that you're so close to blowing; they'll just think that you're very generous. It's a win-win situation!

8. *Patience pays off*
If you're the partner of someone who comes a little too quickly or suddenly, be patient and let them know that you're up for filling your play with plenty of time-outs. Ultimately, edging elongates the time you'll be rolling around naked. And that's a good thing. Always.

"I love knowing that I can control my orgasm if I want to. It has made me much more **confident in bed***"*

The *small* o

How to supersize an underwhelming orgasm Much of the power of an orgasm is influenced by the buildup, and not necessarily the length of the orgasm itself. So if your orgasms feel oh-so-boring rather than oh-so-scintillating, your gaze should be squarely trained on the minutes and hours leading up to the climax as you look to make changes.

First, take stock of your life. Are you running ragged? Stressed at work? Going through family drama? Consider what changes will make space for more satisfying sex. Regular massages at a salon or from a giving partner may help to relax you. Delegating projects at work, or sharing babysitting services with a neighbor, may help cut down on tasks that make you cringe at the thought of yet another thing to do. All of these matter when it comes to getting to a place in your day where you feel like not only do you have time for sex, but you have time for great sex.

Next, consider the time leading up to your lackluster orgasms. Were you rushing around, thinking you might as well have sex since your partner wants it? Because you feel guilty if you don't? That's not a good entrance to sex, is it? Try to only have sex that you want—even if it takes a few minutes of kissing, touching, and licking before you start to want it. It also helps to slow down foreplay. For some moments, close your eyes and focus on how it feels to touch and be touched. During others, open your eyes to take in what's happening. Mindfulness techniques have been shown to help enhance arousal, so try to focus on the scents, sounds, and textures of your sex play as you build arousal.

The term "watching the clock" has negative connotations—as though the only reason you would watch the clock is because you can't wait for something to end. But it can sometimes

Mindfulness techniques enhance sexual arousal, so focus on the *scents, sounds, and textures* of your **sex play**

help to occasionally glance at the clock, as long as it isn't obvious and doesn't take away from the overall experience. If you can steal a glance at the clock when you begin kissing, touching, or going down on your partner, you can make sure you spend at least 5, 10, or 15 minutes doing whatever it is you're doing that feels good to one or both of you. Another tactic is to aim for a certain number of things—for

LET YOUR MIND WANDER If you need more titillating details than you can get in your waking life to keep your excitement bubbling away, **don't be afraid to fantasize**—even if it's about someone who's not your partner, not normally the gender you find attractive, and even (or perhaps, especially) if it's about something you would never do in real life. Sometimes, the more unusual, extreme, or taboo scenes are the ones that will push you pleasantly and explosively over the orgasmic edge. And you don't have to tell a soul about what you dreamed up—unless you want to.

example, 30 slow kisses or 60 sucks on his penis. This can help you stay focused on what you're doing and stay in the moment, which can ultimately make sex wetter, hotter, and more saucy—which matters to your orgasm.

Intensifying your partner's orgasm

A strategy that some people use to help their partner achieve more intense orgasms involves "making" their partner wait and/or beg for more intense stimulation that will result in orgasm. This works well for some individuals, particularly

Dirty talk can help keep your partner **focused on the present moment**

those who find it easy to orgasm and thus don't mind a little waiting game. It can work poorly for others, such as those who find it difficult enough to orgasm without their partner trying to "control" it.

A few additional techniques may work:

- When you're going down on her, if you have a free hand available, massage her breasts.
- During intercourse, make his imminent orgasm more intense by firmly pressing the area just behind his scrotum, which can indirectly stimulate his prostate.
- Use dirty talk to build a scenario in which you're doing something sexy together— make sure you know what your partner's into before you go too far. Dirty talk can keep your partner focused on the moment (never mind that it's a fantasy version of the moment).

over time. During your pillow talk try to get him or her to open up about what they like in bed or what reliably gets them off. We've known lots of people who need a trigger to make it happen: feet in their face, a hand around their throat, a finger in the butt, being called certain names. Before you take responsibility for them getting off, find out if there's something that needs to happen to... make it happen.

Some girls (and guys) don't

I (Grant) recently hooked up with a girl in her early 20s who has never orgasmed with a partner. She has what's termed situational anorgasmia: She

Just because your *trademark move* is suddenly not doing the trick, don't assume that you've **lost your mojo**

can orgasm under some conditions—when she's on her own—but not others. Other people may have primary anorgasmia (in which they've never experienced an orgasm) or secondary anorgasmia (in which they've lost the ability to have an orgasm). There are plenty of treatment options for these conditions, which can include sex therapy, hormonal patches or tablets to correct hormonal imbalances, clitoral vacuum pump devices, and medication to improve blood flow, sexual sensation, and arousal.

Men, too, can experience a similar condition called delayed ejaculation or DE. While most men can bring themselves to orgasm within two to four minutes of intercourse, men with DE might only be able to achieve orgasm after 30–45 minutes or, indeed, it may never happen. Sometimes this is due to stress, lack of sleep, or anxiety about pleasing his partner. Other times, it's due to a man conditioning himself to respond to a masturbation technique that bears little resemblance to actual sex, or it could be a side effect of certain antipsychotic and antidepressant drugs.

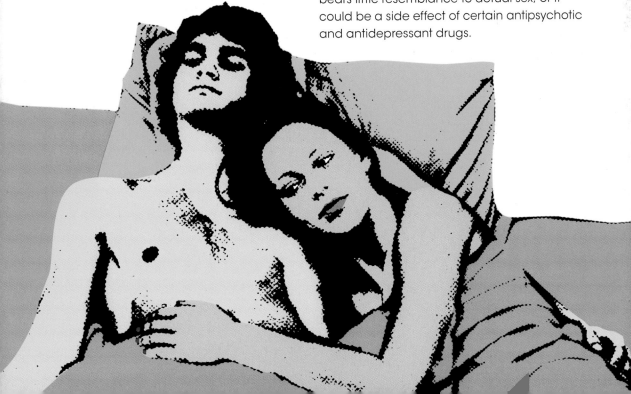

Chapter 8
Afterglow

Sexy *comedowns*

Stay-sexy techniques for afterward Sexy means different things to different people and just as there are many ways to have sexy foreplay, there are varied ways to come down from a great sex high rather than plummet into free fall with a boring or offensive "come and done" strategy. We say linger—even if it's casual sex, it doesn't mean you have to jump back into your clothes and head home without a proper goodbye.

Each of the following have been sexy comedowns to people we've heard from. There's no right or wrong overall—it's a matter of what you feel you can pull off with confidence, what will make you feel like a rock star in bed, and what you think your partner will find so sexy, funny, adorable, or romantic that they'll look forward to the next time you're together.

Cuddle The time-tested favorite of many couples, cuddling is undervalued. Men in particular may reap extra benefits from touching, kissing, and cuddling, whether they're done on movie night on the couch, or as part of sexy afterplay.

Kiss There's no rule that says that kissing is only used to heat things up. Kissing is also a great way to cool things down while still staying connected. The kisses you give one other can stay on each other's lips or travel the length of each other's bodies. We know of one couple who would often kiss each other's genitals after sex, as a way of paying homage to the fantastic sex they'd just had.

Bathe together It's not that sex is dirty, but it can be fun to clean up after sex together—to hop into the shower and wash the parts you've just ravaged. Washing each other gives you both another chance to take care of one

There's no rule that says *kissing* is only used to heat things up. It's also a *great way to* **cool things down**

another, too. And, of course, it provides you with one more opportunity to look at each other in all your naked glory.

Touch Massage is an integral part of afterplay for many couples, whether they're heading to work after morning sex or calling it a very late night after an evening in bed. Some incorporate sex toys that are lying around—vibrators can double as back massagers and feathers can help draw attention to the senses. Don't be surprised if things start to heat back up, though!

CLEAN UP AFTER YOURSELF So you've just used your semen to decorate her breasts and stomach? Grab a warm, damp (not soaking wet) towel and lovingly dab her off. Or, if you're game, **lick it off her** and then kiss (this isn't for everyone, so ask first). Some men lick the vaginas and anuses of their partners after they've come inside them. Others couldn't be paid enough to do so, but to each his own.

Share It can be sexy to relive verbally a few key moments from very good sex. It never hurts to throw in a few "wow, that was good!" or "why don't we do this more often?" comments, or to specifically compliment your partner on a particularly good move—that thing they did with their hips, the way they kissed you for what seemed like forever, or the way they licked you for ages without expecting anything in return. It can also be sexy to just hang out and talk naked in bed. There can be something very vulnerable about being naked together when you're not having sex, and this vulnerability can

lend itself to creating an intense kind of emotional intimacy that can be highly appealing—and often lead to more sex or, at least, more time in bed.

Get creative This has to come from the heart, of course, but we know of men and women who have been so inspired by great sex that they've made up a poem or a limerick on the spot ("There once was a guy with a tasty dick…"). We know of some who have invented songs together that paid tribute to their sex lives in a cheeky or silly way. Some artistically inclined people sketch their partners postsex. Others take out their phones and ask for permission to take a picture. (Some exhibitionists even allow for the posting of these online.) And some hopeful would-be parents start dreaming up baby names. Again—sexy afterplay is a very individual experience.

There is something vulnerable about *being naked together when you're not having sex* that lends itself to **intimacy**

Postsex *etiquette*

Now what? You've been witty, flirtatious, and charming and you've brought your A-game in the sack. Mission accomplished! But now you find yourself naked, covered in goo, sharing a bed with someone whose last name you don't know, and it's awkward. You've been so focused on the performance that you've given little thought to what to do in the immediate aftermath. The following pointers should help smooth things over.

Relish the afterglow If you've been doing it right, you ought to be a sweaty, gooey mess once you've had a thorough session—and probably quite reluctant to move. That's fine. Feel free to bask in the postorgasmic afterglow for a bit, remark on the event with a sincere amazement for what just went down. "Wow" usually sums it up nicely. Even if you don't see wedding bells in your future, don't shirk from cuddling up if the mood strikes you both. Postorgasm, oxytocin is flowing through your bodies and getting cozy with one another will feel especially good. Don't feel pressure to be a chatty Cathy. If there is an awkward silence, a postcoital kiss is a great way to smooth things over.

And guys, the only time you have to snap into action after sex is if you've managed to get a great glob of semen in your partner's eye or in your own. That stuff not only stings but will often make an eyeball bloodshot or, if not cleaned up quickly enough, can even gum eyelashes shut. Not a very smooth finish. If you do get it in somebody else's eye, immediately get up and offer him or her a moistened washcloth. Similarly, if you've shot a load over a partner's face or chest, bear in mind that semen tends to get extremely cool and unpleasant-feeling in seconds. Reach for a tissue and clean up your mess or at least offer to.

remark on the event with sincere amazement for what *just went down*

What next? Most long-term couples don't seem to fret much about postsex etiquette. They probably have a routine (e.g., get breakfast, cuddle, fall asleep, etc.). But those who are newer to having sex with each other aren't often sure what to do after sex. Should they stay? Should they go? Should they go quietly, almost sneak out?

We would like to see more people ask each other what they want to do, and specifically ask the person whose bed they're in ("is it all right if I stay over?" should suffice; if you really don't want to be there, it's fine to say that you have

SECOND THOUGHTS Fleeing the scene before your unsuitable bed partner awakes should always be a last resort. Come on, you're a big boy/girl now! If you simply must tiptoe from their lair, do so knowing that random sex partners do have an uncanny knack for reappearing at the worst possible moment. So really, it's better not to make a habit of vanishing David Blaine–like as the sun rises. It's not becoming of an accomplished sexer like you.

an early morning and need to go). As long as you feel safe and comfortable enough to stay over, it can be a nice experience for everyone involved—even if you don't see yourself dating or marrying this person. If you were drinking the night before, or trying so hard to get into each other's pants that your talk was more sexy than personally revealing, waking up together and grabbing breakfast can be a nice way to get to know one another. Running off or sneaking out isn't about being "independent" or "cool"—

waking up together and grabbing breakfast can be a nice way to **get to know** one another

particularly if your partner feels rejected or like they must not have been good enough at sex to get you to stay. Rather, sleeping together can feel warm in ways that humans don't often get to experience outside of being in a relationship, and can help people feel more human and more connected. So, if you feel welcome and safe, why not stay?

If you had a great time, you can summarize your feelings about the evening's events when you depart. Something like "that was really fun, let me know if you ever want to do it again sometime" works well. It's not exactly aloof but certainly not clingy. In fact, it's sort of sexy. As they see you saunter away they won't be able to help thinking about the amazing time they had with you and wonder, "Where did they learn how to do that?" Don't worry, we won't tell.

However you approach taking stock of your sex lives together, keep in mind that nearly everyone wants to please their partner, and most everyone is trying their best. If something went poorly, they might not understand what you want, so it's time to communicate.

"He could tell there were no fireworks for me and wanted me to tell him what I like, but I was too shy*"*

she thinks...

Some couples talk about sex after they have it—what was good or not so good (if they know each other well and know what their partner's ego can and can't take), what was positively delicious, and what they hope to try another time. Postsex talks have a lot going for them, namely that they're in the moment, right after sex, so both of you can remember what happened and how it made you feel.

If you feel shy talking about sex right after it went down, you still have time in the days that follow. You can text your partner with a sex highlight ("Loved it when you..."), or send him a link to a sex toy or piece of lingerie, with a note about how it might be a fun addition next time.

"I like to remind him *of the best parts, hoping he gets the text in a meeting!"*

If you need to point your partner in the right direction, be positive about what they do well and suggest things that would feel even better. Reserve criticisms for really terrible or painful moves. These should be rare if you've been talking and listening well.

"It's easy to be positive when there's a lot to be positive about! *Every time seems better than the last. He knows now what makes me tick"*

"*I wordlessly guided her into a minor adjustment to her technique (with major impact on me), and very soon* **she got the picture,** *and no one had to get hurt*"

No one likes bad reviews, but sitting through more of her misinformed ministrations won't do anyone any favors. Correct bad form in the moment—guide her hand/mouth/hips to a better location/speed/angle.

When heaping on praise, make it personal and unique to your partner and your experience. There's a subtle yet important difference between "I love having my balls sucked on" and "I loved it when you sucked on my balls like that."

"*She often says she doesn't have a man's body and has no idea how what she's doing to me feels—and that letting her know is* **my job**"

he thinks...

"*You know what they say—if you can't say something nice... but there were lots of* **good things to say**"

If you have to get verbal about it, protect their ego. Let them know what works for you—not what they did wrong—as if you're letting them in on a big secret.

If you've just been taken to sexual nirvana and back, by all means let your guide know all about how they exceeded your wildest sexpectations. In a postcoital haze mention how amazing it felt when he/she did that thing to your thing. We all love a compliment and, besides, positive reinforcement should mean they pack your future sessions with the stuff you gave rave reviews for.

Chapter 9
The sensible part

Good reasons *to* *touch yourself*

Self-examination of your breasts and vulva or testicles Taking care of your precious parts is important, not just for a rocking sex life, but for your health, so self-examination should be something that you do on a regular basis. Most disorders can be dealt with safely and relatively easily if caught early, so at the first sign of a problem, take yourself off to your healthcare provider.

Breast self-examination Getting to know your breasts is an important part of self-pleasure as well as caring for your health. By regularly examining your breasts, you may be able to play a role in the early detection of breast cancer, if you find a lump that feels different than the many normal and noncancerous lumps found in women's breasts. (Young women and those who are breastfeeding may particularly feel a good number of lumps, and some women simply have more dense breast tissue.)

Report any changes in how your breasts feel or look (such as an unexplained rash) to your healthcare provider so that he or she can follow up with a clinical breast examination. And don't be surprised if it's your partner, rather than you, that first finds a lump—often, sexual partners are the first to notice changes in each other's bodies.

Vulvar self-examination Although rarely discussed openly, it is important for women to perform monthly vulvar self-examination. By getting to know your own genitals, you can spot various changes that may be signs of a sexually transmitted infection (STI), a benign skin disorder, or, rarely, vulvar cancer.

BEYOND THE BOYS Checking out your testicles is important—even lifesaving—but it's not the only thing you should visit down there. Men should become familiar with how their genitals look overall. That means checking for anything that looks or feels unusual on the penis or the mons (the hairy triangular area above the penis), too—we're talking sores, pimplelike bumps, etc. Most changes will be benign but it's better to look and report any changes to your doctor.

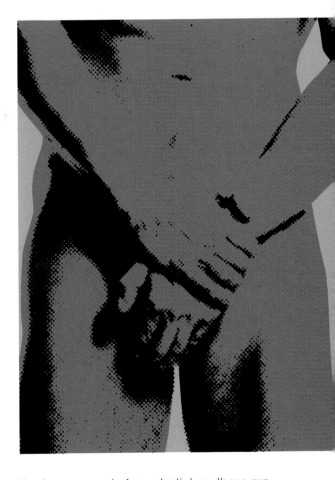

When you examine your genitals, it can be helpful to do so in a well-lit room in front of a mirror, whether it is a full-length mirror, a handheld one, or a small compact (women have different preferences for using mirrors to view their genitals).

Look for changes in color, feel, freckles, or new lumps and bumps and report any changes to your healthcare provider, making sure to mention any changes in relation to chronic itching or irritation. Most changes are not likely to be cancerous but it's better to be safe than sorry, particularly as so many health conditions are more easily treated when caught early.

Testicular self-examination

Unlike many cancers, testicular cancer is more likely to strike men in their prime reproductive years. Fortunately, self-examination has been found to be a helpful strategy for early detection.

You might find it easiest to perform TSE after a warm shower or bath, when the scrotum is more relaxed. Some men actually find it easiest to perform TSE while they're in the shower—or get help from a willing partner who soaps them up and explores their testicles (but don't get distracted from the task at hand!). You'll want to examine one testicle at a time, using your hands to gently roll the testicle between your fingers. With practice, you'll get used to feeling the epididymis (the tubes that carry sperm) at the top rear part of your testicles—these are normal bumps to feel. Feel for any new lumps or bumps on the other parts of your testicles, even if they feel very small to you (e.g., pea-sized or smaller), and also be on the look out for how your testicles feel (swollen/achy/painful?) or look (such as if there's a color change). Although most testicular changes will not be cancerous, they should all be reported to a healthcare provider.

Performing TSE on a monthly basis, or thereabouts, can help you become more comfortable and familiar with what's normal for you—how your body looks, feels, what's normal, and what's not. Report any changes to your healthcare provider, even if you think it's nothing serious. Better safe than sorry!

Spotting *something sketchy*

When genitals go wrong (thrush, phimosis, vaginitis, etc.) The genitals are body-part superstars. They allow us to go to the bathroom, make and deliver babies, and have the kind of orgasmic sex that sends shivers down the spine. But sometimes, things go wrong. Below are listed a few difficulties that plague people's precious parts—in some cases, commonly; in others, more rarely.

Thrush Yeast infections are common among women and, unfortunately, can lead to itching, discomfort, and painful attempts at having sex. If you have a yeast infection and would like to have sex, you need to let your partner know, and you need to be a little creative about it. Perhaps you could go down on your partner who could return the favor by holding a vibrator against your clitoris, giving you a sensual massage, or doing something else that doesn't cause you vaginal pain. Communicate, be creative, and seek help from a healthcare provider.

Research shows that most women don't diagnose their own yeast infections accurately, so unless you experience recurrent yeast infections, you're better off phoning a nurse or doctor to describe your symptoms than rushing to the drug store for home treatment, which may worsen your genital discomfort.

Phimosis This condition occurs when a man's foreskin is so tight that it cannot easily be retracted to reveal his glans penis (head). In adults, phimosis may be caused by a number of things, such an infection, scar tissue (resulting from injury), or chronic inflammation as may occur from some skin conditions, such as lichen sclerosus. Phimosis can lead to very painful erections.

Men who have difficulty retracting the foreskin should seek advice from a healthcare provider. He or she may recommend either gentle stretching of the foreskin, topical medications or, less commonly, circumcision or other procedures.

Vaginitis There are several different types of vaginitis, or vaginal infections. Some can result in painful sex. Others can result in an unpleasant odor. Women who notice a fishy odor coming from their vagina, or who have chronic vaginal itching, burning, or irritation should mention these symptoms to a healthcare provider. Women and men whose female partner has a strong vaginal odor may find themselves in the difficult situation of wondering if or how to broach the topic. If you generally have a good relationship, you may be able to break the news gently by saying how difficult or awkward it is for you to say this, but you care about her, have noticed this odor, and wonder if it might be something for her to talk about with a healthcare provider.

Vaginal and vulvar pain Many women experience genital pain. For some, it's an ongoing issue that results in pain during daily activities (such as riding a bike) and/or during sexual activities.

There are many different causes of genital pain, including allergies, medication side effects, benign skin conditions, and pain disorders. Women who experience genital pain should speak to their doctor or other healthcare provider.

Painful ejaculation Although it is uncommon, some men experience pain when they ejaculate. This may be caused by orchitis (inflammation of one or both of the testicles), prostate gland problems, or may even be a side effect of taking certain medications. Men who experience painful ejaculation should always bring this to the attention of their healthcare provider.

Peyronie's disease This is a condition in which hard lumps or plaques form inside the penis. Because of the way in which they develop, this can result in a scar that reduces the elasticity or flexibility of the penis and results in a penis that has a significant curve or bend to it when erect. Although many men have a natural curve to their erect penis, men with Peyronie's disease can have a more extreme bend or curve, as well as some pain.

Sometimes the plaques go away without treatment. Other times, the problem becomes quite severe and gets in the way of men's sex life due to the pain or due to finding it difficult to maneuver the body into sex positions that both partners enjoy. If the problem does not resolve on its own, medical treatments are available including injections and, if needed, surgery. Your healthcare provider will be able to guide you in the right course of action for you.

Viral infections

Signs, symptoms, and treatments Viral infections are with you for life and have no known cure. For that reason, try not to get them or give them. These lifelong ailments can be treated and suppressed, however—and don't need to spell an end to your adventurous sex life. An early and accurate diagnosis is going to be a huge help when it comes to managing them.

Herpes This often begins with an initial burning sensation that may alert you to the presence of small red bumps around the genitals or anal area. These bumps then turn into clusters of small blisters and, later, sores. The initial outbreak after infection may be the most severe—giving you headaches, fever, painful urination—but the intensity and frequency of outbreaks tends to decrease over time. Herpes is more easily transmitted before and during flare-ups.

People with herpes have an average of around four outbreaks per year, with each one lasting around one to two weeks. If you have blisters or sores, it's important to go see a doctor while they are still there so that a swab can be taken and a diagnosis confirmed. After the sores have gone, testing for herpes becomes more complex and less reliable.

Condoms won't ensure that you don't get or give herpes, but they can reduce the risk. Stress, fatigue, and poor diet can increase the occurrence of flare-ups and there is medication that can suppress outbreaks, shorten their stay, and greatly reduce the risk of transmission.

Genital warts Genital warts are a manifestation of HPV or Human Papillomavirus. The warts themselves—when visible—can look like small pimples or cauliflower-like lesions around the genitals or anal area and are generally painless. Because they can occur in areas not covered by a condom, they can still be spread even when you rubber up.

If you do have genital warts they can be burned, frozen, or removed with a scalpel by a doctor or urologist, but they may reoccur. Topical medications are also available and often no treatment is needed (they frequently go away on their own).

Your suspected genital wart may just be an inflamed hair follicle (folliculitis), a skin tag, or a pimple. Get it checked out and know for sure. Also, over-the-counter wart treatments are not made for this purpose and should not be used.

Hepatitis A and B If you like eating ass—and really, who doesn't?—you are putting yourself at risk of contracting Hepatitis A and B. Symptoms include flulike illness, a pain in the

COMMON INFECTIONS Around **20 percent of the US population has genital herpes**. Many people don't even know they have it and are unlikely to be diagnosed, so continue passing it on without realizing it. **HPV is the world's most common STI.** There are over 100 strains. Most types are asymptomatic and benign, but types 6 and 11 account for over 90 percent of genital wart cases. Types 16 and 18 are linked to cervical, penile, and anal cancer.

gut, dark-colored urine, and jaundice. The good news is that you can actually get vaccinated against Hepatitis A and B with a combo vaccine that lasts for up to 12 years, though it's still smart to get screened every five years or so.

Hepatitis C Unlike Hepatitis A and B, Hep C can't be currently vaccinated against. Compared to other STIs, contracting Hep C through sex is considered rare, although couples in which one person is positive are advised to use condoms. Vaginal penetrative sex is believed to have a lower risk of transmission than sexual practices involving higher levels of trauma (such as fisting or anal sex). Most people suffer no symptoms upon infection—it could be years, even decades, before being diagnosed.

HIV/AIDS So, this is the one that you really don't want. It's with you for life, you're contagious from the moment you have it, and symptoms might not show up for about 10 years, meaning that if you don't know that you have it—millions don't—you could infect a lot of people. You should have an HIV test at least once a year if you are involved in any activity that can spread it. Which, if you're having sex, you are (ask your healthcare provider for a more personalized risk assessment and testing recommendations). Fortunately, condom use can greatly reduce the risk of passing HIV during oral, vaginal, and anal sex.

Symptoms of AIDS include weight loss, fever, fatigue, muscle aches, extended periods of diarrhea, swollen lymph nodes, skin rashes, and easy bruising.

HIV is too big and important a topic to be discussed fully on this page, but there is plenty of information around and many different resources available. Ask your healthcare provider to point you in the right direction.

Bacterial and parasitic infections

The knowledge on little nasties STIs aren't super sexy, but knowing about them can add to your sexy factor. If you're ignorant about STIs, you're unlikely to know how to get tested or respond to a partner with an STI history. Armed with knowledge, you'll be better positioned to be empathetic when a partner shares their STI history with you—and better able to be forthcoming about your own STI experiences.

Bacterial infections

Chlamydia Many men and even more women don't show symptoms of having chlamydia, but those who do will have them materialize within five days to three weeks of infection. Women may notice burning during urination, painful sex, low-grade fever, nausea, and/or a smelly, yellowish discharge from the cervix. Men can experience a watery, milky discharge from the penis; heavy, achy-feeling balls; and may also feel like they're pissing hot lava—I (Grant) had this one myself and would like to ensure you that it's no pleasure cruise.

It's especially important to get routinely checked out for chlamydia if you want children as, left untreated, this infection can lead to infertility for both sexes.

Gonorrhea 80 percent of women and 10 percent of men who have gonorrhea don't show symptoms. Women who are lucky enough to get the signs that something is up can expect a yellow-green vaginal discharge, pain during sex, tenderness of the vulva, and painful peeing. Men—who are much more likely to show symptoms—may have a puslike discharge from the urethra and a burning sensation during urination.

Like chlamydia, gonorrhea can cause sterility in both men and women if left untreated, and can also increase the chances of ectopic pregnancy and miscarriage. Your job is to get tested at least once per year and anytime you have unprotected sex with a new partner.

Syphilis Up until about 100 years ago, getting syphilis could mean going mad, having your internal organs eaten away, disfigurement, and death. Nowadays, penicillin can clear it up right quick. You just have to take your symptoms to a doctor.

The first symptom you're likely to notice is a chancre (a pea-sized ulcer) on the spot where the bacteria entered your body: genitals, anus,

COMMON INFECTION Chlamydia is the most common bacterial infection in the US, UK, and many other countries. **People under the age of 25** are most likely to be infected. About half of men and most women who have the infection experience no symptoms.

mouth, breast, or even fingertips. After a while the chancre will heal but the bacteria is still growing inside your body. Later, you could experience flulike symptoms, hair and weight loss, and grayish white sores in your mouth. From here on in, it gets even worse: tumors on the bones and under the skin, blindness, mental incapacity, and even death. You won't have to worry about any of that, however, because you've got the good sense to be tested for syphilis on a regular basis, right?

Parasitic infections

Crabs If you find that you are super itchy around the genitals and anus you might have crabs or, to call them by their proper name, pubic lice. It usually takes about five days after transmission for you to start clawing at yourself and you may also experience a mild fever and a general malaise.

You don't even have to have sex to get this one; infected bedding, shared towels, and borrowed clothing will occasionally do the trick.

Treatment comes in the form of a specialized shampoo for pubic lice and will knock these little bloodsuckers out pretty quickly. However, if you want to make sure that you or the people you live with don't get a second dose, commit to washing and heat drying all of your clothing and sheets, and giving your home the most intense spring cleaning it's ever seen.

Scabies Very similar to a pubic lice infection, these little jerks burrow through your skin, excreting eggs and poo as they go. Charming. The presence of scabies may be signaled by the appearance of little reddish-brown bumps on your skin, although you may not actually get the itching or bumps until well after you catch scabies, sometimes up to a month. Like crabs, they can be knocked out with an over-the-counter medicated shampoo, throughly washing your clothes and sheets, and a good spring cleaning.

Trichomoniasis Often called "trich" and pronounced "trick," trichomoniasis is a common STI that affects both men and women, although symptoms are far more common among the fairer sex—and men rarely even realize they have it. Trich can be passed through penile-vaginal sex or vulva-to-vulva sex. Most men who have trich have zero symptoms. If they have any at all, they're often limited to mild irritation inside the penis, slight discharge, or burning. Women, however, more commonly notice symptoms including a strong vaginal odor. The good news is that trich is usually easily cured with antibiotics, so check in with your healthcare provider for more information or testing. As far as prevention goes, condoms win again— hands down—for their role in preventing trich.

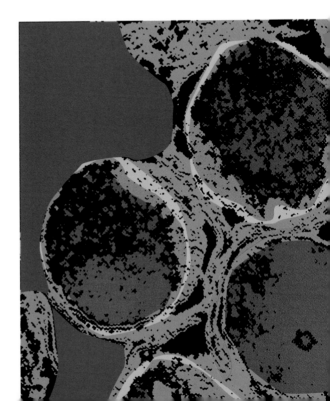

I've got something *to* *tell you...*

How to break the news that you have something you can't shake If you have a sexually transmitted infection (STI) for which there is currently no cure, such as genital herpes, HPV, or HIV, then you need to speak up and let your potential partners know BEFORE you have oral, vaginal, or anal sex with them—or any other kind of sex play, such as dry humping, that might possibly transmit the infection.

Curable STIs If you have an STI such as chlamydia, gonorrhea, or syphilis, it's time to take a brief sexual time out until you've fully completed a course of treatment and had a follow up visit with a doctor to ensure that you're good to go.

Although they might be temporarily unpleasant and uncomfortable, sexually transmitted infections such as these can almost always be knocked out with specifically designed antibiotics.

Having the conversation Unfortunately, there is currently no cure for certain STIs, such as genital herpes, HPV, or HIV, and if you have any of them, you'll need to inform every partner you have from now on about it before he or she has got their mouth or genitals near your bits and pieces.

There's no use trying to make it sound sexy because, well, it's not. That said, by informing your potential partner, you will be demonstrating that you care about their wellbeing enough to have a tricky, awkward conversation. That should earn you some kudos, no matter what.

I (Debby) often remind my students that one of the best ways to walk into an STI conversation is to get themselves tested as often as recommended by their healthcare provider, and to know their status. This makes it much easier to say something like, "We should have the awkward STI conversation now—I've been tested and I have A but not B, C, or D..." (filling in the blanks, of course, with whatever your STI status is). "Have you?"

By being up front about the fact that you've been tested, you show potential partners that you're responsible and that STI conversations are a normal part of being a great potential sex

GRANT'S SEXPLOITS I contracted chlamydia from a lady I hooked up with casually and, admittedly, not safely. When I told her she had infected me, it turned out she didn't know she had chlamydia, but was aware she had herpes, which she had neglected to mention. I underwent further testing and was thrilled to discover I had only caught one easily treatable STI from her. The experience affirmed my belief in being frank—preferably before rubbing genitals.

partner. And by being honest about any STIs you might have, you help to destigmatize STIs—which might encourage your potential partner to be just as honest with you if they have any STIs as well.

It helps to be knowledgable about STIs, especially the ones that you have, and to share this knowledge with your potential mate. Herpes, for example, can either be transmitted when someone is having a breakout or during asymptomatic viral shedding, and transmission is greatly reduced by taking antiviral medications. Condoms don't prevent transmission but they definitely decrease the chances of contracting it. If you have genital warts and your potential partner doesn't, you can talk about how condoms can reduce but not eliminate the risk of transmission. You can

By being *up front* about the fact that you've been tested, you show potential partners that **you're responsible**

also suggest they talk with their healthcare provider about Gardasil, the HPV vaccine that can be used by both women and men to reduce the risk of genital warts.

By knowing this stuff and honestly telling a potential partner what's up, you're empowering him or her to make an informed decision. If they ultimately decide that the risk of contracting herpes or HPV is one that they're not willing to take, respect their decision, and take solace in the fact that you've behaved responsibly. Not only is it the right thing to do—it will be greatly appreciated!

It's nowhere near the end of the world
Finally, don't let anyone make you feel bad about having an STI—the vast majority of women and men have HPV, even if they don't know it (and most men don't know it due to limited testing abilities). And about one in four or five adults has genital herpes—but again, most don't know it. At least you know it, are adult about it, and can share information about risk reduction and how you can still have amazing sex, with or without an STI.

References

page 12

1. Meston, C.M.; Frohlich, P.F. (2003) *Love at First Fright: Partner Salience Moderates Roller-Coaster-Induced Excitation Transfer.* Archives of Sexual Behavior, 32(6), 537–544.

pages 18–19

1. Dixson A.F.; Halliwell, G.; East, R.; Wignarajah, P.; Anderson, M.J. (2003). *Masculine somatotype and hirsuteness as determinants of sexual attractiveness to women.* Archives of Sexual Behavior, 32(1), 29–39.

2. Singh, Devendra (1993). *Adaptive Significance of Female Physical Attractiveness: Role of Waist-to-Hip Ratio.* Journal of Personality and Social Psychology, 65(2), 293–307.

3. Tracy, J.L.; Beall, A. *Happy Guys Finish Last: The Impact of Emotion Expressions on Sexual Attraction.*

page 24

1. Reece, M.; Herbenick, D.; Schick, V.; Sanders, S.A.; Dodge, B.; Fortenberry, J.D. (2010). *Condom use rates in a national probability sample of males and females ages 14 to 94 in the United States.* Journal of Sexual Medicine, 7 (suppl 5), 266–276.

page 30

1. Heiman, J.R.; Long, J.S.; Smith, S.N.; Fisher, W.A.; Sand, M.S.; Rosen, R.C. (2011). *Sexual satisfaction and relationship happiness in midlife and older couples in five countries.* Archives of Sexual Behavior. Published online ahead of print, January 26, 2011.

page 40

1. Herbenick, D.; Schick, V.; Reece, M.; Sanders, S.A.; Dodge, B.; Fortenberry, J.D. (2011). *The Female Genital Self-Image Scale (FGSIS): results from a nationally representative probability sample of women in the United States.* Journal of Sexual Medicine, 8(1), 158–166.

Herbenick, D.; Reece, M. (2010). *Development and validation of the female genital self image scale.* Journal of Sexual Medicine, 7, 1822–1830.

Herbenick, D. (2009). *The development and validation of a scale to measure attitudes toward women's genitals.* International Journal of Sexual Health, 21(3), 153–166.

page 53

1. www.physorg.com/news10824.html

page 56

1. Giles, G.G.; Severi, G.; English, D.R.; McCredle, M.R.E.; Borland, R.; Boyle, P.; Hopper, J.L. (2003). *Sexual factors and prostate cancer.* BJU International, 92(3), 211–216.

2. http://www.telegraph.co.uk/education/5806691/NHS-tells-school-children-of-their-right-to-an-orgasm-a-day.html

page 68

1. Seal, B.N;, Bradford, A.; Meston, C.M. (2008) *The Association Between Body Esteem and Sexual Desire Among College Women.* Archives of Sexual Behavior.

page 74
1. www.thepornreportbook.com

page 83
1. Levin, R.; Meston, C. (2006). *Nipple/breast stimulation and sexual arousal in young men and women.* Journal of Sexual Medicine, 3(3), 450–454.

2. Miller, S.A.; Byers, E.S. (2004). *Actual and desired duration of foreplay and intercourse: discordance and perceptions within heterosexual couples.* Journal of Sex Research, 41(3), 301–309.

page 88
1. Hughes, S.M.; Harrison, M.A.; Gallup Jr., G.G.; (2007). *Sex Differences in Romantic Kissing Among College Students: An Evolutionary Perspective.* Journal of Evolutionary Psychology, 5(3), 612–631.

2. http://www.reuters.com/article/2008/04/07/us-bug-responsible-bad-breath-found-idUSTON77980320080407

page 90
1. Kinsey, A.C.; Pomeroy, W.B.; Martin, C.E.; Gebhard, P. *Sexual Behavior in the Human Female.* Philadelphia: W. B. Saunders Company.

2. Levin, R., Meston, C. (2006). *Nipple/breast stimulation and sexual arousal in young men and women.* Journal of Sexual Medicine, 3(3), 450–454.

Tairych, G.V.; Kuzbari, R.; Rigel, S.; Todoroff, B.; Schneider, B.; Deutinger, M. (1998). *Normal cutaneous sensibility of the breast.* Plastic & Reproductive Surgery, 102(3), 701–704.

page 143
1. Kanner, Bernice. (2003). *Are You Normal About Sex, Love, and Relationships?* 52.

page 144
1. Herbenick, D., Reece, M., Schick, V., Sanders, S.A., Dodge, B., and Fortenberry, J.D. *An event-level analysis of the sexual characteristics and composition among adults ages 18 to 59: results from a national probability sample in the United States.* Journal of Sexual Medicine, 7 (suppl 5), 346-361.

Index

Acknowledgments

AUTHORS' ACKNOWLEDGMENTS
We would like to thank our wonderful agent, Kate Lee, for helping *Great in Bed* come to life. In addition, we are most grateful to our editors (Daniel Mills, Laura Palosuo, and Emma Maule) for their patience and perseverance as we passed drafts of our book back and forth across the pond. We would also like to thank our publisher, Peggy Vance, for her vision and for pairing us together for this project.

Debby would like to thank her colleagues, whose support of her creative endeavors means the world to her: chief among them are Michael Reece, Vanessa Schick, Brian Dodge, and the amazing team of talented graduate students at The Center for Sexual Health Promotion at Indiana University. She is also grateful to her colleagues at IU's The Kinsey Institute, most notably Jennifer Bass, Stephanie Sanders, Julia Heiman, and Catherine Johnson-Roehr, whose encouragement is never-failing. Further, Debby is full of thanks to her family and friends - particularly James – who listened to Debby mull over multiple versions of Great in Bed during the writing of it. And finally, Debby cannot thank Grant Stoddard enough – for his hard-won wisdom (though frankly much of it sounds like it fun), his candid and clever writing, and for keeping her in stitches throughout the process.

Grant would like to thank to Dr. Debby for backing up his hunches and observations with some science and Aki for reading through various drafts and giving her input. He would also like to thank—and in several cases sincerely apologize to—those who have assisted in his research.

PUBLISHER'S ACKNOWLEDGMENTS
Dorling Kindersley would like to thank Angela Baynham for proofreading, Marie Lorimer for indexing, and Adam Brackenbury for retouching advice.

PICTURE CREDITS
The publisher would like to thank the following for their kind permission to reproduce their photographs:
(Key: a-above; b-below/bottom; c-centre; f-far; l-left; r-right; t-top)

2 Corbis: Emely / Cultura. **4-5 Getty Images**: pbnj productions (c). **6 Getty Images**: B2M Productions (c). **10-11 Corbis**: Image Source. **13 Corbis**: Ocean (tr). **15 Getty Images**: Joshua Sheldon (cr). **16 Corbis**: Image Source (tl). **21 Getty Images**: B2M Productions (cr). **23 Getty Images**: Stone / Uwe Krejci (cb). **25 Getty Images**: Image Source (cb). **27 Getty Images**: Ghislain & Marie David de Lossy (br). **29 Corbis**: Vincent Besnault (tr). **50 Getty Images**: Brand X Pictures / PNC (tc). **51 Corbis: Creasource** (br). **73 Corbis**: John Turner (br). **76 Getty Images**: Photographer's Choice / B2M Productions (ca). **79 Corbis**: Blue Images (cr). **82 Getty Images**: Stockbyte / George Doyle (ca). **143 Corbis**: Tom Grill (cr). **159 Getty Images**: Microzoa (cr). **161 Getty Images**: Microzoa (cr). **165 Getty Images**: Joselito Briones (bc). **166-167 Corbis**: Beyond. **169 Corbis**: Beyond (cb). **171 Getty Images**: Steven Errico (bc). **174-175 Getty Images**: Jose Luis Pelaez Inc. **176 Getty Images**: Peter Dazeley (br). **181 Corbis**: Juan Fariña (cr). **183 Science Photo Library**: Pasieka (br). **185 Getty Images**: Jose Luis Pelaez Inc (bc)
All other images © Dorling Kindersley
For further information see: **www.dkimages.com**